ISBN: 978-1-940087-51-1
21 Crows Dusk to Dawn Publishing, 21 Crows, LLC

Always follow the rules/regulations in the areas you explore. Do not trespass. Do not enter areas after dark if it is not allowed—most parks are open dawn to dusk, but check times before entering. The information in this book like addresses are given to show where the story is located. Please check property ownership before visiting. QR codes and GPS guides were added to many trails so you can click on them with your phone camera and view the route. These routes may change or perform differently on different phones, so check for updates before relying on these solely.

Table of Contents—

Tennessee Cont'd

West Virginia Cont'd

Maryland

Pennsylvania

Pennsylvania Cont'd

Ohio

Citations

A few things to know—

*I hiked all the areas in this book; some I returned to a second time because of seasonal closures. I learned a good lesson and I will pass it on to you—**check for the most updated map of the hiking location online before visiting and call the controlling agency if you can—**there are many factors in the blink of an eye that can change the course of a trail system like fires or inclement weather. The maps I add in the book are for a general idea of the trails; each does not outline intricate details or daily updates. The types and quality of the hiking areas in this book vary widely from road beds to rugged paths to well-maintained nature trails. There are all types of hikers, so there are all types of trails including driving and wheelchair accessible.*

I use the terms below to describe each to give you a better idea of what you are getting into when you hit the trail. Always check ahead of time for trail closures due to seasonal weather-related hazards. I assume if you are searching out haunted hikes, I do not need to warn you about the risks associated with exploring for ghosts on or off the trail. Do not go on trails after dark in unsafe areas or trespass on private or public areas during off-hours.

Types of Trails:

Out-and-Back—Begin and end at the same location, returning along the same route. Typically day hike trails.

Loop—Begin and end at the same location, but follow a trail/trails that form a loop. Typically day hike trails.

Point-to-Point—Begin and end in different locations, usually for long-distance, extended trips for backpacking. Typically multiple-day hiking like the Appalachian Trail.

One-Way—Trails maintained in a loop and developed, for the safety of the natural area and hikers, so that hikers can only go one-way from start to finish, unable to turn to go in the opposite direction. Seen often in cliff areas where it is unsafe to pass or areas with protected wildlife species/plants to maintain minimal human interference.

Spur—Trail that branches off a main trail and leads to a dead end, usually at a point of interest such as an overlook or historical feature.

Quality of Trails:

Developed Trails—Man-made paths wide enough to comfortably hike with grass and brush typically removed. Features are usually added such as steps, ramps, and bridges. They require routine maintenance.

Multi-use Trail—Used by pedestrians but may also be used by bikers and horse-back riders.

Backcountry Trail—Not maintained and usually have no features like restrooms or camping facilities. Used by experienced hikers.

Nature Trail—Routinely maintained and usually offer interpretive signs along the path.

Trail Road—Unpaved lane or road that vehicles may use.

Rail-trail—A paved or graveled trail made from an abandoned railroad corridor/tracks.

A Few Elements to Heed When Hiking Abandoned/ Remote Places:

I added QR codes to many trails so you can click on them with your phone camera and view the route. These routes may change or perform differently on different phones, so check for updates before relying on these solely. The time the mapping system stated it would take me to get from one point to the next was rarely the same amount of time it took me to hike the trail—it took me longer.

- When old buildings are abandoned, sometimes old outhouse pits and wells are not covered and the brush grows up around them. Watch where you step!
- Mark your starting location on your positioning and mapping devices before you hike in case you get lost.
- Leave an itinerary of your travel destinations with someone before you depart.
- Bear, elk, and large predators share the same paths as humans. I have seen many on or near the trails that are in this book. I kept my distance and gave them the right of way. Be aware of your surroundings so you do not stumble into their path and startle them. But also be conscious of the fact that they may sense you long before you realize they are there.

Virginia

Appalachian National Scenic Trail: George Washington National Forest—Punchbowl Shelter & Ottie Powell Marker

Monroe, Virginia
Amherst County

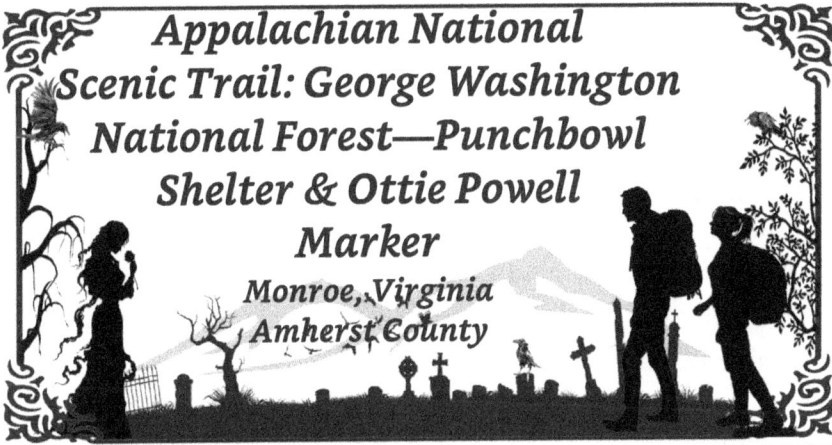

Little Lost Ghost of Bluff Mountain

Blue Ridge Parkway—Image: Library of Congress

The Blue Ridge Parkway is a National Parkway meandering 469 miles around the peaks of the Blue Ridge Mountains through Virginia and North Carolina. It connects two parks, Shenandoah National Park and the Great Smoky Mountains National Park. If you drove it from start to finish at the leisurely-paced speed limit of forty-five miles per hour, it would take about 11 to 12 hours, without a break, to complete. That said, most do not mind the long excursion.

They are not in a hurry. They take the trip for the many views and overlooks. Some stop and hike the trails, including the Appalachian Trail, which crosses its path. And a few more adventurous come to check out a ghost – that of a little boy who haunts a mountain ridge along the Appalachian Trail in George Washington National Forest in Virginia. His story goes like this—

Edwin "Ed" Powell was a farmer in the late 1800s who shared property with his brother James near Pera, Virginia, along Dancing Creek, a stream which, for a short time, parallels the parkway and can be seen from the Dancing Creek Overlook should you drive there. He was also a circuit-riding German Baptist Brethren preacher in the Blue Ridge Mountains. They were called Dunkards or Dunkers because they believed in fully immersing or dunking those baptized. He and his wife, Emma Belle, had eight children, and among them was a four-year-old boy Emmet. He was tall for his age with fair hair and complexion, blue eyes, and a full forehead. He had the habit of sucking the forefinger and middle finger of his left hand.

The rugged mountain area where the Powell family lived—

He was probably doing just that when he left with his brothers and sisters for their usual 1-mile walk from home and west to their schoolhouse on a particularly chilly and gray cloudy morning of November 9, 1891. The scent of an oncoming rain hung in the air. As Emmet passed his father, who was husking corn that day, the four-year-old stopped and bade him stay so he could help. One must wonder if Ed Powell's eyes lingered on his son's with any trace of foreboding because Ed had a strange dream the night before. In it, he watched as a black undertaker's wagon pulled along a road. It stopped, and the reverend had walked to it and climbed inside. An old man was reclining in the rear of the wagon who said, "This is my house." There was also a foot-long casket in the wagon with no lid, and above it, a tiny light floated seemingly on its own. Ed Powell had awakened with a start from the nightmare, telling his wife what he had seen. After, he could not fall back to sleep. If it was a warning, a premonition of what was to become, the minister could certainly not have deciphered whatever clues it offered. So, Ed denied Emmet's request, and he told the boy his teacher expected him to be at school each day like his siblings. Little Emmet shuffled away with his brothers and sisters.

The children attended a one-room schoolhouse, Dancing Creek School, with 25-year-old Nannie Ann Gilbert as their teacher. It was a typical day with students of varied ages and grades all attending to lessons and learning under one roof and from one teacher. As was customary, the girls took a five-minute recess in the afternoon. When their break was over, the boys were then allowed time to play outside. Miss Gilbert then asked the boys to collect large twigs and branches for the pot-bellied stove before returning to the schoolhouse.

There was a forest of chestnut, oak, and pine trees surrounding the small building. The boys set out in the chilly air to collect the wood, some working a little farther away as they had already collected the choicest burning wood near the schoolhouse in the earlier weeks after a long cold spell. The boys boisterously returned with their collection in the middle of the girl's lessons and were told to sit so Miss Gilbert could continue the schooling. In the chaos of unpacking the firewood from arms to stove and floor and resuming the school day, it was not for twenty minutes that it was noted the youngest in the classroom had not returned. Without delay, Miss Gilbert peered outside and, after seeing no Emmet, sent the boys back out to the area they had collected the firewood. When they could not find the little one, she sent the children to Emmet's home and the homes of nearby neighbors, but no one had seen the child.

Now a trail, left, runs through the mountains but when little Emmet Powell disappeared, it was thick with nearly impenetrable brush, saplings, and stones.

Soon, everyone in the community and even outside areas joined the search. They stationed able-bodied men around the rises and valleys, hoping that they would hear him calling out. Night came upon them, and cold rain turned to slushy snow at the higher peaks. Many were exhausted. Some went home. But Henry Wood, a neighbor, had an old hunting hound much-cherished by the boy, and the two had become fast friends. Wood sent the pup to seek him out. The dog was gone for hours before returning, and later, many wondered if Wood's old hound dog had come upon the boy and stayed with him.

Hundreds took up the search over the following days. But all they discovered was a half-mile trail where young Emmet had dragged a 12-foot chestnut branch intended for the fire. Unfortunately, however, his path had led away from the school instead of toward it. Confused and left behind by the older boys, the four-year-old had gone the wrong direction. Eventually, all gave up save Ed Powell, who continued searching whenever he could, hiking into the mountains still seeking out his boy. When rumors began that the boy could have been kidnapped, Emmet's father offered a reward for his return.

It was not until nearly five months later, on Sunday, April 3, that four young men were traveling along the trails of Bluff Mountain when one's dog went astray. Its persistent barking compelled the men to the top of the peak. As they crested the summit nearly three and a half miles from the schoolhouse where Ed Powell's son disappeared and stopped just short of a large stone, they beheld the tiny, lifeless body of a child lying on his back, one arm outstretched and the other missing. There was little flesh left on the corpse, and his feet were separated from his body. But by the raggedy clothing torn by scrubby branches and thorns and left to rot in the weather, they knew they had found Emmet Powell.

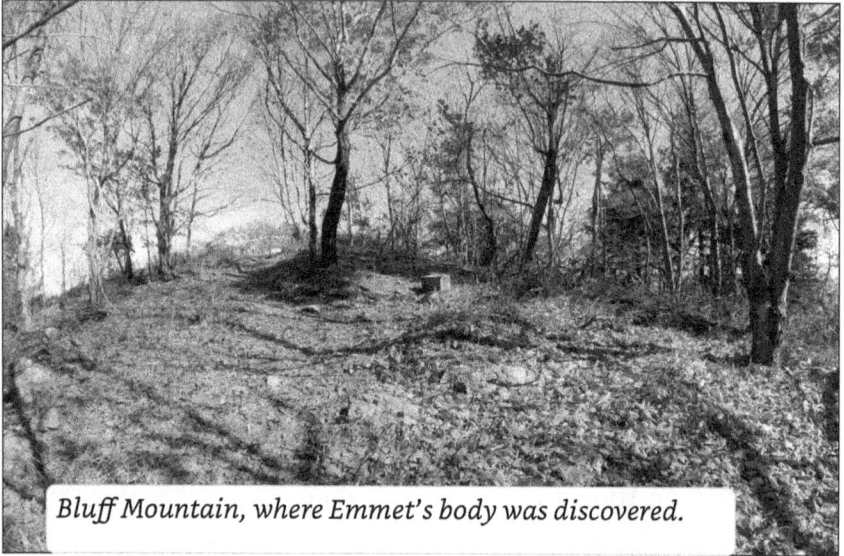

Bluff Mountain, where Emmet's body was discovered.

A doctor who examined the body said the little boy probably laid down to rest on that first night at the summit. After falling to sleep, he died of exposure. Little Emmet was buried once in the cemetery by the school. His father later reburied him by his home. Years would pass, and his fateful journey was made famous by J.B. Huffman's story where he called the boy "Ottie" and used the proceeds to build a monument where the little boy died. Later, the Appalachian trail was constructed to cross the summit of this mountain, and it passed by the memorial.

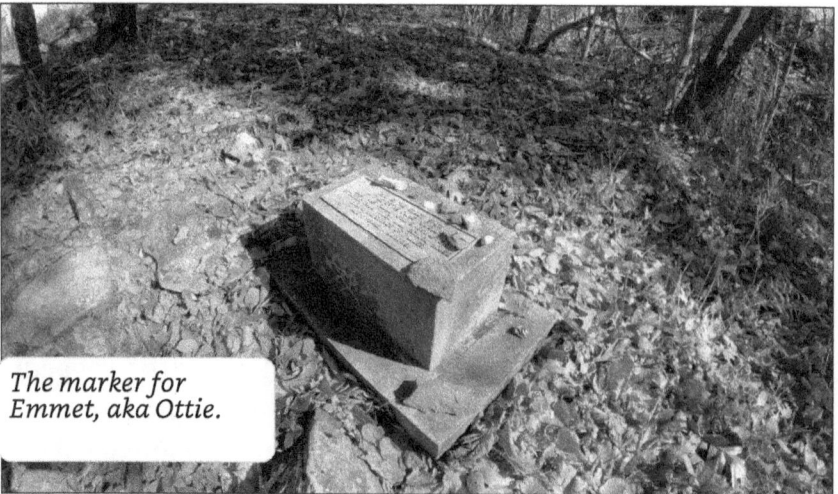

The marker for Emmet, aka Ottie.

Punchbowl Trail Shelter—

A shelter camp, Punchbowl Trail Shelter, was built not far away so those taking the long trail could stop for respite for the night. It was then that more hikers came to the area that whispers of a ghostly boy visiting the trail and shelter began to occur. He is witnessed standing near the camp, whimpering, before wandering away and trudging through the thick brush near the place where he laid down to rest and passed away.

Parking: Punchbowl Mountain Overlook Pull-off on the Blue Ridge Parkway (37.673973, -79.334564)

You will cross the road to get to the small path of the **Appalachian Trail**—(37.674167, -79.334382). It is marked with a wooden post.

Standing in the Punchbowl Mountain Overlook pull-off with arrow pointing to wooden post marking the trail.

The rugged Appalachian Trail hiking to the "Ottie Powell" Marker—

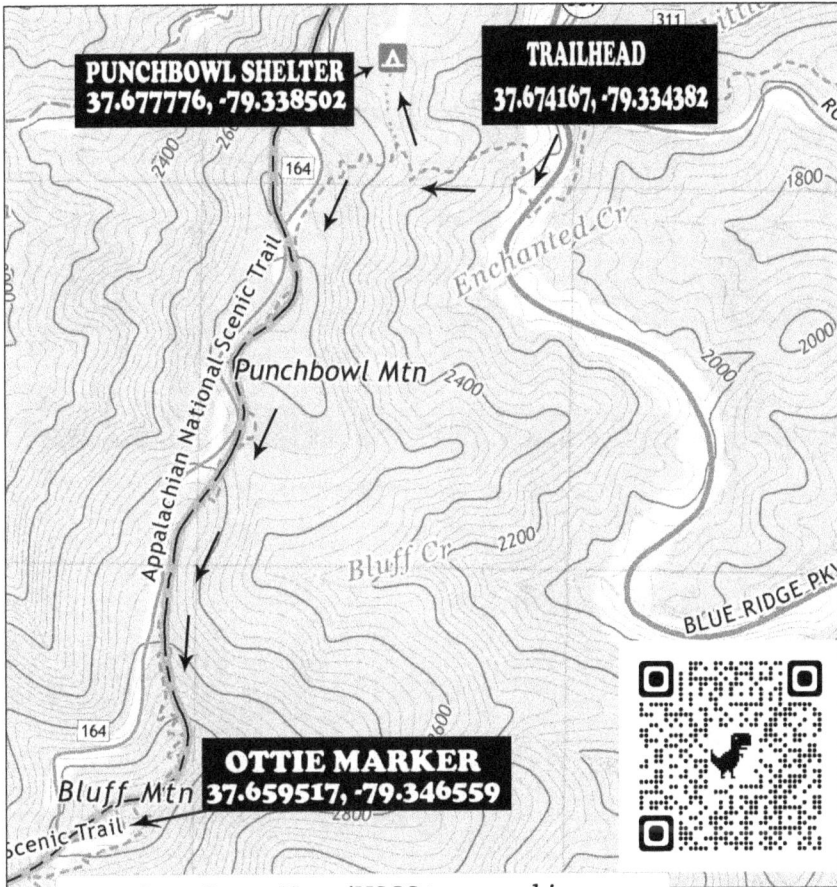

Map: Open Street Maps/USGS topographic maps.

Trail: 2.2 mile hike (one-way) **along the Appalachian Trail** where hikers have witnessed the ghost of the little boy wandering. It also includes taking the spur to Punchbowl Shelter (37.677776, -79.338502) and the location that campers have seen the ghostly boy. Ends at Ottie Powell Marker where the child was found—

(37.659517, -79.346559)

Strenuous hike all uphill on the way there (grueling), and hike down on the way back. Out and back.

Shenandoah National Park: Potomac Appalachian Trail Club—Corbin Cabin Trail
Nicholson Hollow
Madison County

The Company

George Corbin Cabin in Shenandoah National Park—Beautifully restored and maintained by Potomac Appalachian Trail Club—

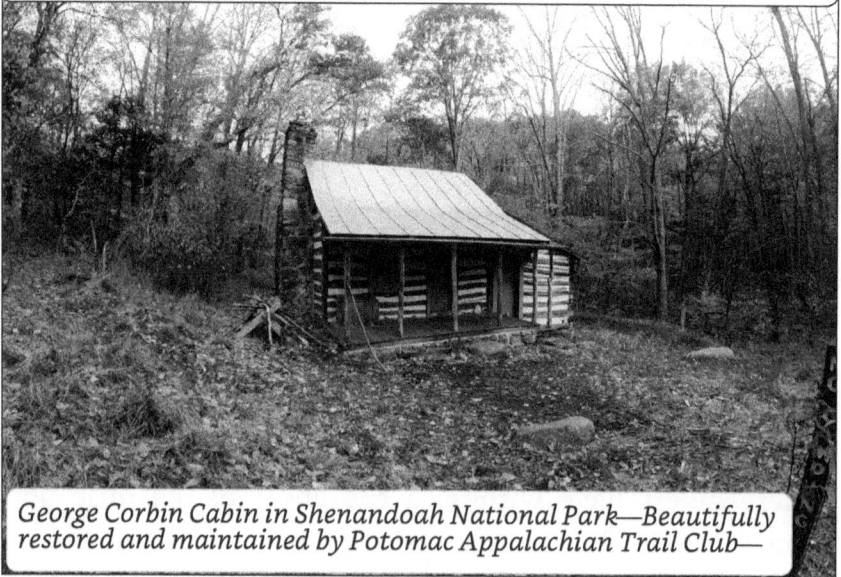

Stony Man is the second-highest mountain in Shenandoah National Park, and the Hughes River flows from its slopes, downward and deep, to a valley called Nicholson Hollow, now a lush and remote forest. It was not always secluded. This hollow was home to a community of homesteaders who lived by farming, grazing, apple growing, and distilling. George Corbin resided there, a mountain farmer who built a cabin when he was 21-years-old by the Hughes River. It was close to his father's home.

George's place was two stories with a single living room downstairs and a single upstairs room and the perfect place to live, love, and raise a family.

George would live most of his life in the hollow. He married three times; his first wife Mildred died before he built the cabin, and his second wife Bertie passed away in the home in February of 1924, only three hours after the birth of their third child. As years passed, a kitchen and other areas were added to his cabin, George married Eula Nicholson, then in the 1930s, the Corbin family was forced to vacate as the land was going to be a part of the Shenandoah National Park.

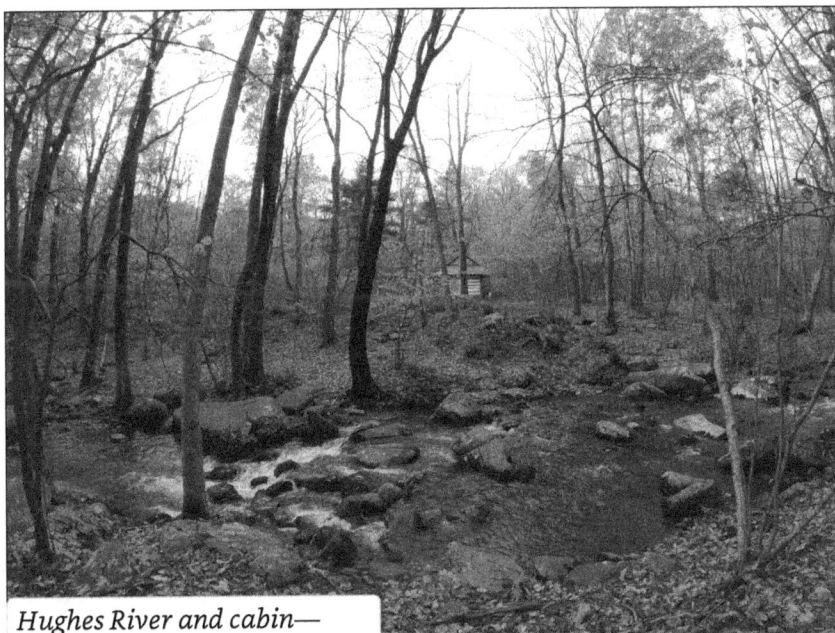

Hughes River and cabin—

The cabin is one of the few that somehow managed to survive the razing of many homesteads in the park. Now the volunteer group Potomac Appalachian Club maintains and rents the Corbin Cabin as one of 43 cabins so folks can get a taste of history, enjoy the outdoors, and experience what it was like to live in the mountains in earlier years. I had heard the old cabin was haunted, but the stories were vague.

Some believe it is George's dead wife Bertie who now comes back a makes a racket when folks visit. It was a cold winter's day when she passed. The doctor had driven to the closest road, and George had waited for him at the path to his home with his horse and brought the man down. All seemed fine, but when George came back from returning the doctor to his vehicle, he found his wife lifeless. He buried her in the frozen ground of the cemetery near the house, then walked four hours to Nethers to get the baby milk. Is it she who makes a ghostly presence? Or is it the groans of an old home making noises, the bangs of a nosy wild animal bumping around the building, or the babbling creek chattering?

Being the adventure junkie I am, I decided to visit the house in mid-November to see if I heard or saw anything. Those who know me understand I am not a "ghost hunter," the type who goes out antagonizing ghosts with rude confrontations and with loads of newfangled equipment. I like the folklore, the stories, and sitting back and letting spirits come to me if they wish. And occasionally, they do.

The Corbin Cabin trail—

Often, I have found that this approach and just a camera make for more encounters. Although I will admit, fiddling with all the scientific equipment is just plain fun.

Regardless, I do not know why I picked that time of year; I do not particularly like camping or renting a non-electric cabin in the winter. The only heat available at Corbin Cabin is a pot-belly stove that needs to be fed wood all night and barely warms a small kitchen area. But after a drive and with backpack tossed over my shoulders, hand warmers tucked into my pocket, and a flashlight, I headed out.

Getting to Corbin Cabin from the parking area is along the same rugged trail that early homesteaders busted through the mountain, so it is narrow, rocky and rugged, and straight down on the way to the cabin and narrow and straight up on the way out. And at the end of the trail before you can get to the cabin, hikers have to cross the modest Hughes River by a series of steppingstones. In the dark, I fumbled around on the trail, traversed the water without incident, and even saw a bear before it saw me and ran off into the forest.

Once inside, I set my flashlight down on the floor laid out my sleeping bag on a couple of blankets right in front of the stove. To set the mood for the cabin stay, I played a bunch of old Bluegrass songs while I got toasty warm. Finally, I went to bed at about 9:00 or 10:00 in the silent and dark air. There were no lights but the meager fire, and just as I laid down, I saw a shadow like a man leaning against the doorway between the two rooms, and a voice said quite clearly: "Dee, I think we've got company." I shot up, thinking for a half-second that I'd gone to the wrong cabin, then quickly remembered I had a key that unlocked it. I was not scared, just startled. I lay there for a while, stoked the fire, and fell into a deep sleep. (And by the way, I am not sure who "Dee" is when I heard the voice. But it was clearly that name.)

Sometime during the night, I was awakened by: "Ma'am?" I worked my way up on my elbow, thinking I had dreamed hearing the voice. I noticed the fire was out, and it was chilly, so I added some more wood. There was a lot of banging going on outside, which I figured was a bear as it was too large for raccoons, so I laid back down and enjoyed the bumps and bangs of the woods until I fell asleep.

Again, I was awakened to a chill in the air and a "Ma'am?" I opened my eyes, looked around, and realized I must have been asleep for a couple of hours because the fire was out again. I stoked it up and tried to fall back asleep. Now it was really cold out that night and dark. I took a walk to the outhouse outside with my cell phone light blazing and did not see anything amiss. I returned, was fully awake from the brisk walk, and as I lay there, it sounded like three or four people were trekking past the cabin. I looked at the time, and it was about 2:00 in the morning. I thought it odd that someone was hiking this late in the dark on a trail that was a 4 to 5 mile loop, but I listened to their chatter for the longest time, and then they faded away.

Stoking the stove.

So, the night progressed as such—each time the fire went out, I was awakened by that "Ma'am?" I would estimate it was 4 or 6 times. Had the voice not roused me in the fifteen-degree night, I would have been darn frozen when I awakened in the morning. But it did. And I stayed cozy and warm all night.

I assume Mister Corbin haunts the home, and I appreciated his gesture in not allowing me to freeze to death that night. Those who knew George Corbin said he was a pleasant and friendly man. I think that perhaps he was caring too. And I am glad he and his family were kind enough to share his old homestead with me, this stranger who made herself comfortable within without an invitation from them. I also hope when I go back, they treat me as kindly again.

———————————————————————

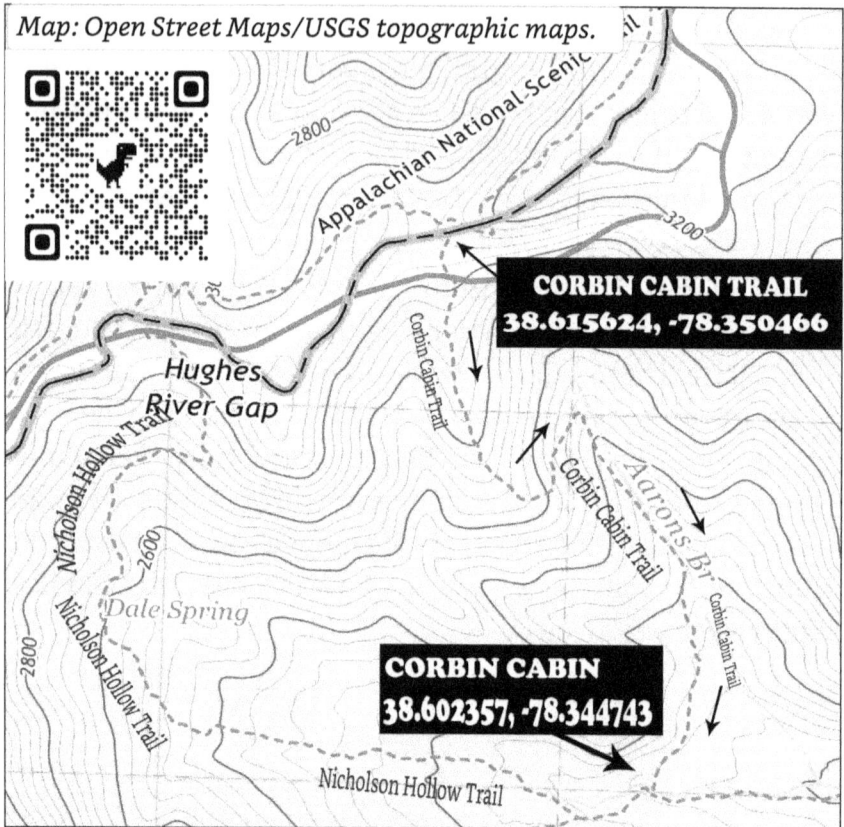

Map: Open Street Maps/USGS topographic maps.

CORBIN CABIN TRAIL
38.615624, -78.350466

Hughes River Gap

CORBIN CABIN
38.602357, -78.344743

Parking: Corbin Cabin Cutoff Parking (you can rent the cabin or just hike the trail to the cabin)
Luray, VA 22835 *There is a fee to get into the park.*
(38.615810, -78.350587) To get to the trail, you have to walk across a road. Trailhead is marked by a cement post.

Trail:
Trailhead: (38.615624, -78.350466)
Hike to Cabin and back: 1.4 miles (one-way) Steep. All down hill in, and a strenuous hike back out. Out and back.
Cabin: (38.602357, -78.344743)

Corbin Cabin Hollow, Nicholson Hollow and Appalachian Loop: 4.2 miles. You can also continue along Nicholson Hollow Trail for a loop trail. Just after crossing the Hughes River (on the cabin side), you will see the Nicholson Hollow Trail. The climb back toward Skyline Drive is steep before you reach the road. Take a left on Skyline Drive for about 70-75 yards. You will see a spur trail that will take you to the Appalachian Trail marked by a cement post. Go right, which will take you about a half-mile, and to the parking lot.

Appalachian National Scenic Trail: Sarver Hollow and Sarver Hollow Shelter Spur Trail

Newport, Virginia
Montgomery County

Spending the Night With the Wild and Dead

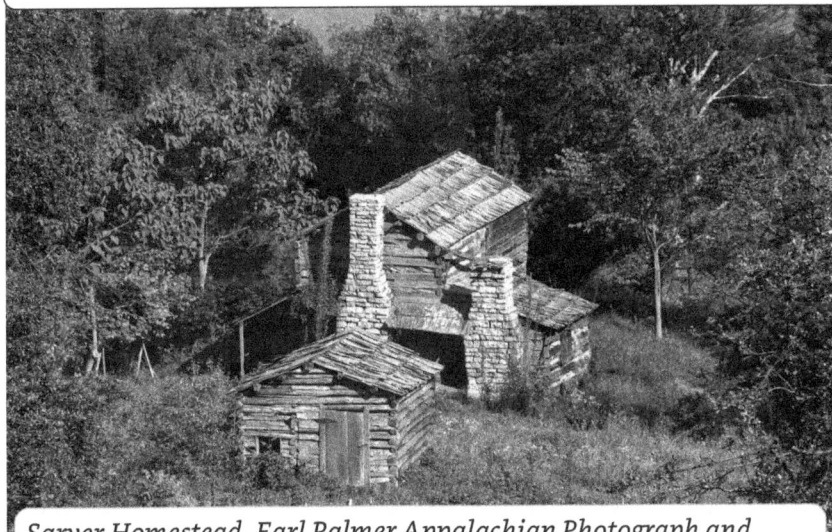

Sarver Homestead. Earl Palmer Appalachian Photograph and Artifact Collection, Ms1989-025, Special Collections and University Archives, Virginia Tech, Blacksburg, Va.

They were just a family like any other, making a living off the land in the mid-1800s through part of the 1900s. Henry and Sarah Sarver, with help from Henry's brother-in-law and wife (James and Elizabeth Elmore), built a two-story cabin about 1859 in a hollow beneath the Sinking Creek Mountain. Not long after, both men went to war, Henry joining Company C of the 22nd Virginia Regiment in May of 1861.

Only Henry returned after surviving a Union prisoner of war camp at Point Lookout in Maryland when captured in the 3rd battle of Winchester in September of 1864. James died at Pickett's Charge in Gettysburg, and his wife Elizabeth and her son came to live at the Sarver's homestead.

Like other settlers in the region, the family moved large amounts of stone to expose the soil beneath and farm the rugged land covered with rocks. With these stones, they built fences to form barriers against foraging animals for the family's cultivated crops (mainly corn and garden vegetables), sheep pens, apple or peach cribs and made foundations for the home and outbuildings. Some were just neatly stacked high and tall as they had no use for them close by. When they were finished clearing the brush, trees, and stones, the homestead sat on tidy hilly farmland with several babbling creeks.

Stacked rocks found throughout the area were not Indian burial mounds as some have guessed, but instead stones carefully piled to make fences or pasture.

The Sarvers lived the typical life of mountain farmers through the Civil War and the Great Depression, well over seventy years. In the mid-1950s, the last family members, elderly and needing to be closer to town, abandoned the farm. The family's shelter against the rain, sleet, and winds eventually collapsed to years of harsh mountain weather and a fallen tree. Only a rough wood skeleton crumpled on the ground with two high chimneys, outbuilding, stacked rock, cemetery, and spring reveal that a family once lived, loved, and died there. Of course, and occasional ghostly appearances.

The remains of the Sarver Home—

The Appalachian Trail runs not far from the old Sarver homestead (at about mile 681 from the southern terminus) as it courses its way 2190 miles in length. This trail is marked by white paint blazes on trees. There is a clean and comfortable Appalachian Trail overnight shelter and privy there maintained by the Roanoke Appalachian Trail Club.

It is called Sarver Shelter, and marked by signs and side-trail blue blazes. It is a steep, rocky hike down into the hollow thick with trees. The shelter and the old homestead have hosted not only weary hikers but also ghosts. For years, hikers have mentioned that when staying at the Sarver Shelter (or at the old homestead before the roof fell), they heard distinctive footsteps coming toward them or were awakened by someone shaking them. Others mention hearing voices when nobody else is around.

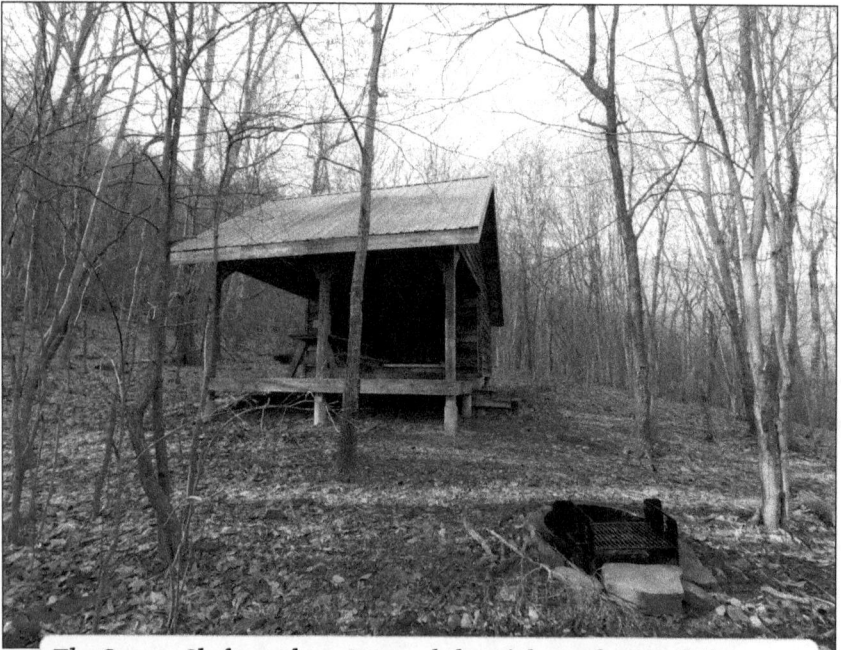

The Sarver Shelter where I stayed the night and many hikers have heard mysterious sounds in and around the building.

When I backpacked a section hike, I stopped at the Sarver Shelter and stayed the night; it was incredibly windy with 44 mile-per-hour gusts and I was lucky to have the place to myself. Afraid of falling limbs, I set up my tent inside the three-walled lean-to. It was late winter/early spring, dusk around 6:00 p.m.

I hiked around until the oozy darkness consumed me, then I took the trail from the homestead toward the Sarver Shelter and when just about to the spring, I heard a child's voice call out, "Mom?" Being a mom, I instinctively turned around, expecting a little boy or girl to be standing there. There was nobody. I wrestled with the idea it could be a ghost or a bird or animal call, then sighed and headed back.

The outbuilding next to the home—(you can see this little building in the historic picture—)

Many wild animals wander the Sinking Creek Mountainside—raccoon, deer, opossum, fox, and the occasional bear. I think I had all of them stop for a curious visit near the shelter after dark, including a rather annoying couple of Barred Owls who decided to fight out their territory with each other, hooting, hollering, and cackling most of the night. I do not know what time the strange things began to happen. I rely on my cell phone for just about everything from mapping to noting the time.

The old spring—I found an old, old tin cup down in the mud while getting water probably left there years ago for passersby and family to grab a quick drink!

My cell phone battery died five minutes after setting up camp, and with my typical scatter-brained luck packing, I left the cord to my charger sitting in my jeep somewhere. After the rugged hike, I expected to fall right to sleep but just lay there contentedly listening to the wind, watching the clouds roll beneath the sliver of moon as the cover to my tent blew off immediately. Maybe three hours of staring and begging for sleep went by when I finally felt my eyes close. Then, knock-knock! I was awakened by the rap of knuckles to wood right next to the wall I had set up the tent. My eyes opened wide, and I looked around, thinking that perhaps other hikers had found the shelter. Not so. The building was devoid of anything but me.

I waited a few seconds, then nervously flicked on my charger flashlight and swept it around the darkened area of the shelter. Nothing. (Well, there was one dreadfully horrifying moment—inside the shelter, hooks are dangling from the ceiling to hang backpacks and other sundry items.

As my beam of light fell on one corner and a hook, I could make out a man floating there wearing coveralls and holding something that looked like an ax. I took in a gasping breath before I realized that the coveralls were my coat and the ax, a roll of toilet paper fish-hooked above.) Regardless, when I laid back down again, I was glad I was alone, so nobody heard my traumatized intake of breath. Again, I lay there awake, but this time I could hear, fairly well, the padding sound of footsteps walking around. Then between bursts of wind when the hollow was subdued for about 5 to 10 seconds, I could make out the sound of bells similar to the type sheep dangle around their necks and music like a guitar or banjo playing somewhere below the shelter. Three more times, the knock-knock patted on the wood next to me.

My fearless protector on this trip—who slept through all the bumps, bangs, and ghostly/wildlife activity.

Throughout the night, I heard a bear pass by and white-tailed deer gingerly stepping on the rocks into the camp.

In addition, there were foxes barking, Barred Owls hooting, and a raccoon chattering and sniffing around. I brought my dog Harley with me, a mixed mutt of Labrador, shepherd, and God-knows-what descent. My usual companion, Lucy, an aged, but usually level-headed Golden Retriever, was recuperating from a rattlesnake bite she got hiking with me a week earlier. (*In the snake's defense, it was innocently basking on a warm patch of gravel when Lucy pounced on it, chased it down into a pile of leaves, and tried to dig it out. The poor snake did not declare it a skirmish until the latter.*) I was unsure how an untested Harley would react if other hikers, wild things, or ghosts interrupted our sleep or followed us along the trail.

As it turns out, Harley did quite well—she slept through the animal noises, the wind, and the ghostly happenings. Throughout the night, the knock-knocks continued, and we both fell to sleep to footsteps still rambling around and perhaps a ghostly get-together in the ruins of the homestead below. Honestly, barring the five seconds I was sure an alleged axed murderer was hovering above my tent they did not scare me—they were a family just like my own at one time, eking out a living off the land. It is just that now, they are—dead.

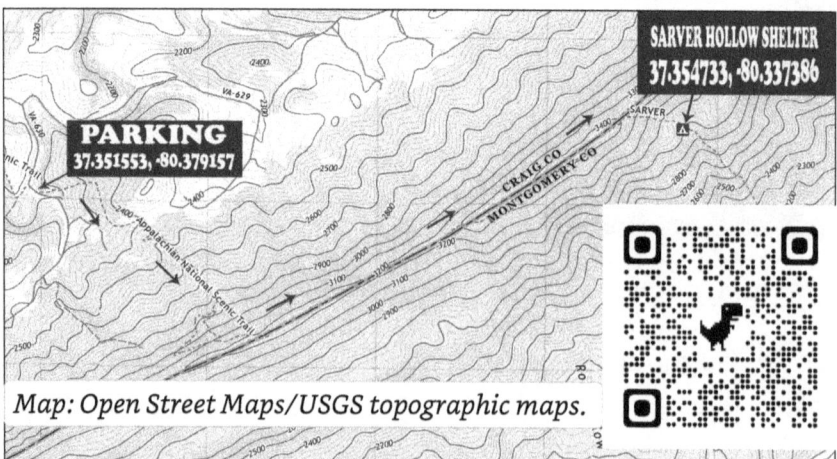

Map: Open Street Maps/USGS topographic maps.

Parking: Grassy area with wooden fence. You will see a gate to your right when you pull in. This is the location to begin. After 0.4 miles, you will pass the Keffer Oak, one of the largest trees on the Appalachian Trail. Northside Road Newport, VA 24128 (37.351553, -80.379157)

Parking area—and arrow showing trail gate and path to follow—

Trail: 3.4 miles (one-way). Out and back. The first 1/4 mile is gentle up and down. The next mile is a strenuous, uphill ascent until hikers reach the ridge. The ridge is about 1.6 miles of mostly flat trail. Once hikers see the trail sign for Sarver Hollow Shelter, it is about 1/4 steep, rocky hike to the shelter and not far after, the ruins of the homestead.

Sarver Hollow Shelter: (37.354733, -80.337386) *If you plan on hiking sections of the Appalachian Trail and staying in shelters, you must register as an A.T. Section Hiker with the Appalachian Trail Conservancy. Applications are online.*

Homestead: From the shelter, follow the wooden signs/blue blazes toward the "spring," and continue onward.

Trail is carefully marked and easy to find. This is the sign that shows the trail turnoff to Sarver Hollow Shelter—

Tennessee

Big Ridge State Park

Big Ridge State Park is about 25 miles from Knoxville. Hikers can trek over 15 miles of trails from deep hollows, to old roadbeds and lakeshores. There are homesteads nearly hidden in the forest and brush along with many cemeteries.

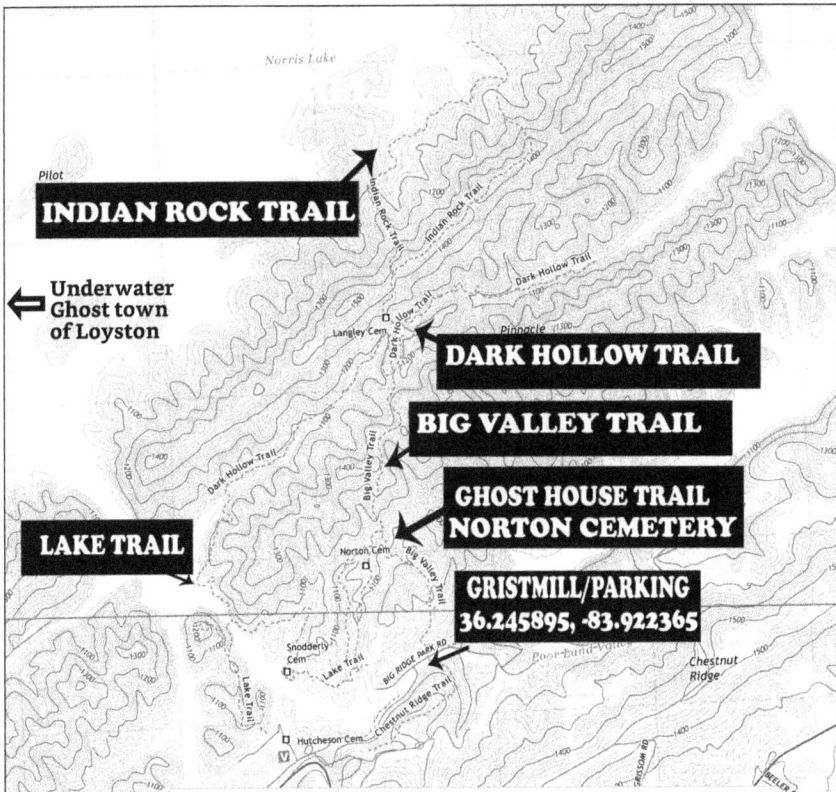

INDIAN ROCK TRAIL

Underwater Ghost town of Loyston

DARK HOLLOW TRAIL

BIG VALLEY TRAIL

GHOST HOUSE TRAIL
NORTON CEMETERY

LAKE TRAIL

GRISTMILL/PARKING
36.245895, -83.922365

Map: Open Street Maps/USGS topographic maps.

Big Ridge State Park— Trail Parking
Maynardville, Tennessee
Union County

Little Girl in the Gristmill

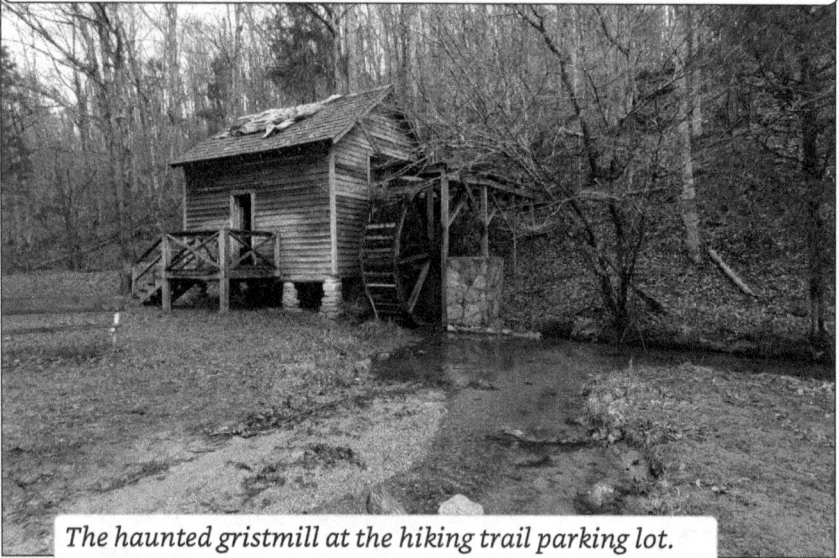

The haunted gristmill at the hiking trail parking lot.

In 1825 Tink McCoy built a gristmill for grinding dried corn into meal along Lyons Spring Branch and later turned the business over to Lewis Norton and his sons. The communities around the mill thrived—corn was a primary staple of early settlers' diet and used in such everyday foods as cornbread and grits. During harvest times and when crops were hauled by mule or oxen-driven wagons, the mill was a popular hub for farmers and their families to gather.

However, in the 1930s and with the creation of Norris Lake, the mill was moved by the Civilian Conservation Corps, and workers used parts to build a replica at Big Ridge State Park not far from the entrance.

During the late 1970s, Fred Flatford was a ranger at Big Ridge. One of his duties involved making safety rounds throughout the park, including the buildings. Flatford's usual method of checking the gristmill after dark was pulling his vehicle up to the building and shining the headlights on the front so he could easily see inside the front door and all around the building. While patrolling one evening, he discovered a little girl squatting in one corner of the gristmill crying. When approached, she told Flatford that she could not find her father and was lost. The ranger took off his jacket, gently wrapped it around her shoulders to warm her, and told her he would return in a moment. Basked in his headlights, he immediately went to his cruiser and radioed his supervisor, who chuckled softly, "We've heard this one before. Don't worry—she's no longer there."

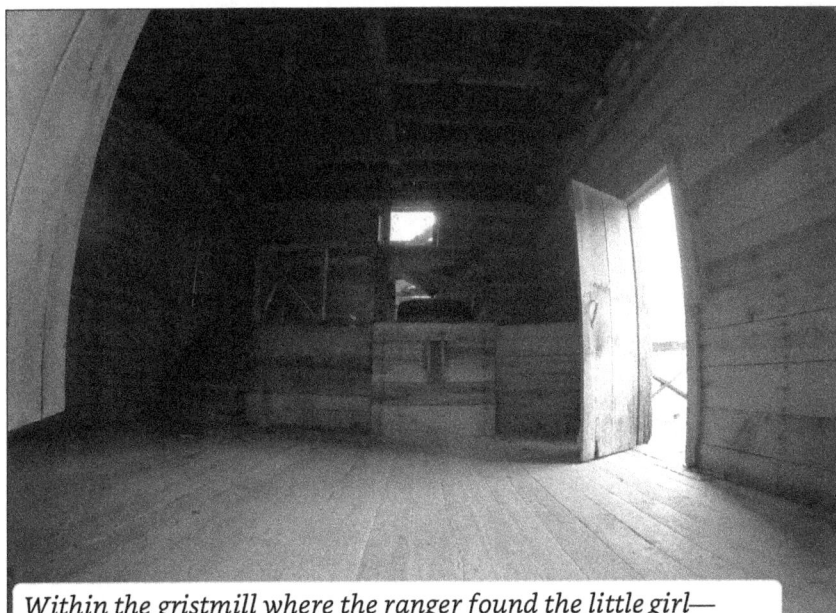

Within the gristmill where the ranger found the little girl—

Undeterred, Flatford returned to the gristmill knowing good and well the little girl could not have fled as he had kept his eyes on the door the entire time he had been at his cruiser. But when he passed the threshold of the door, the child was nowhere to be found. Yet the jacket he had wrapped around her shoulders was lying askew on the floor.

The Norton Gristmill is located at the larger of two adjacent parking lots that are starting points for many of the Big Ridge State Park trails including the network trails of Big Valley Trail, Ghost House Trail, Big Valley Trail, Dark Hollow Trail, and Indian Rock Trail. A short walk across the street and along the service roadway will take you to the haunted hiking areas.

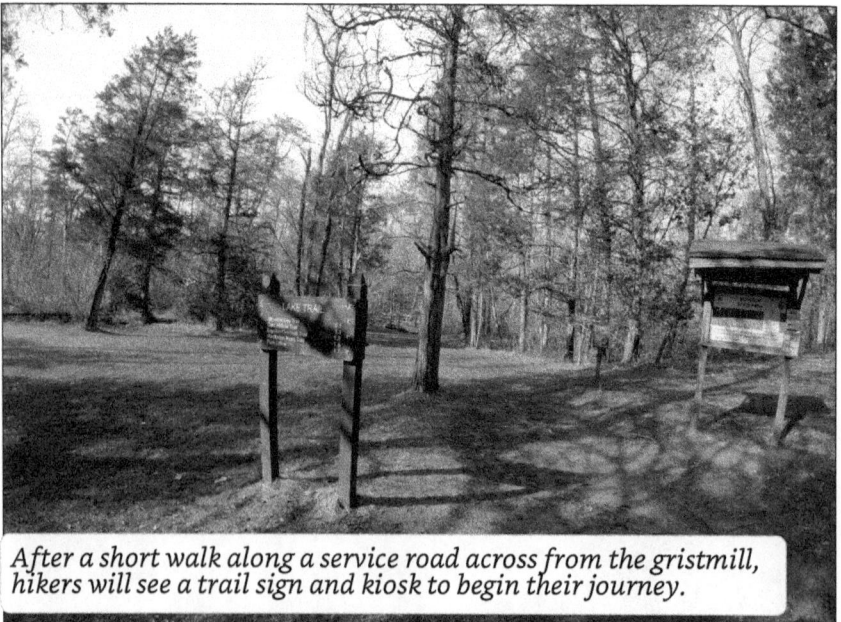

After a short walk along a service road across from the gristmill, hikers will see a trail sign and kiosk to begin their journey.

Parking: Big Ridge State Park Gristmill and Parking
Big Ridge Park Road
Maynardville, TN 37807
(36.245895, -83.922365)

The marked trails that lead past the haunted sites along with historic cemeteries.

Haunted Trails accessible from Gristmill parking area:
- Ghost House Trail: 1.2-miles
- Big Valley to Dark Hollow Trail: 4.8-miles

Big Ridge State Park—
Big Ridge Group Camp/Road to Lake Trail
Maynardville, Tennessee
Union County

Faded Plaid Shirt

The service road leads from the parking area to the trails and group camp and is home to a wandering ghost.

In the mid-1970s and during the winter, a ranger was in the vicinity of the group campsite near the Lake Trail trailhead at Big Ridge State Park. A man, dressed in a faded plaid shirt and dark work pants, sauntered into the camp near the parking lot and roadway. The ranger called out a friendly, "Hello!" Oddly, the greeting was not returned.

Instead, the man slipped away into the woods as if he had not heard anything at all.

The incident so disconcerted the ranger, he later jotted down a description of the stranger, and as he did, something stood out that made him recall a report he had received less than a year before. A church organization had stayed at the group campsite the previous summer. During their visit, several of the campers called out to greet a man cutting through the site. He strangely refused to acknowledge anyone in return. Instead, he disappeared as he walked into the woods. The ranger took in a deep gulp as he recollected the story the campers had related to him—the strange man was dressed in a faded plaid shirt and dark work pants!

Parking :
Big Ridge State Park Gristmill and Parking
Big Ridge Park Road
Maynardville, TN 37807
(36.245895, -83.922365)

Trail: Hike the service road past the trailhead and kiosk to the **Group Camp parking area**:
(36.247999, -83.923878) 0.3 miles from the Gristmill and after passing the kiosk for the Lake Trail and Ghost House Trail.

Big Ridge State Park— Dark Hollow Trail
Maynardville, Tennessee
Union County

Shades of an Old Dark Road to the Underwater Town of Loyston

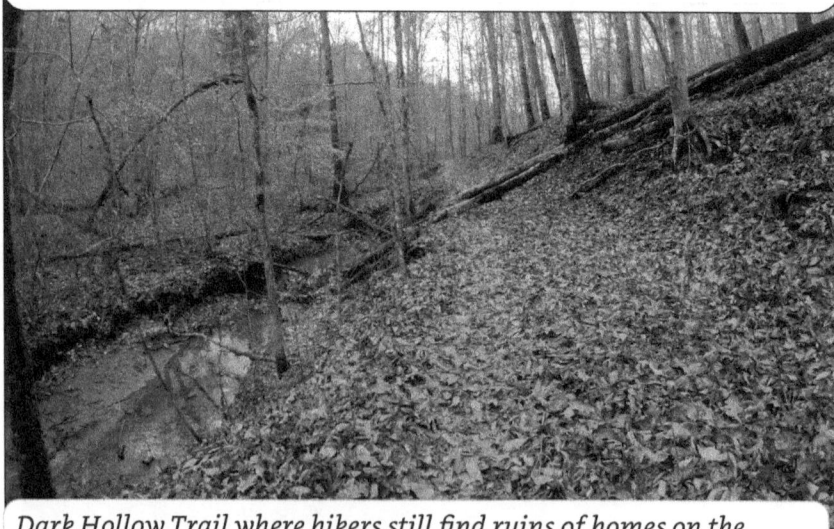

Dark Hollow Trail where hikers still find ruins of homes on the shores of the creek—along with ghostly echoes of the land's past. Those who traveled this old road in days gone by told that it was so narrow and dark that a lantern was needed to light the path.

There is an old road that runs through Big Ridge State Park. It has long earned the name of Dark Hollow Trail, for it is deep within a valley and thick with forest. Nowadays, the road has been cut off on each end by Norris Lake, forcing an eastern and western side.

Ghost town of Loyston before being flooded by Norris Lake and now underwater. Right is George Fox's filling station and general store—

Years ago, residents took this path to travel from one community to the next or deliver their corn to the mill. Many a wagon and later cars and trucks worked their way through the shady glen near the town of Loyston, and along its rugged route, there were small homesteads here and there. Still, people avoided the backroad of Dark Hollow if they could. It is haunted—the air becomes chilly in small pockets, even on hot days, and shadows lurk behind, leaving some to find themselves looking over their shoulder only to catch a glimpse of a black silhouette vanish quickly. Occasionally, park employees and hikers have been startled by the noise of an old car rattling and grumbling, bumping and jarring its way along the old road, but it never passes them or materializes!

Glimpses into the past—belongings of those who lived along the road.

Langley Cemetery just off Dark Hollow Trail—

Parking:
Big Ridge State Park Gristmill and Parking
Big Ridge Park Road
Maynardville, TN 37807
(36.245895, -83.922365)

Trail: There are two sections of trail—
–**Eastern Section**—A 1.3-mile trail that begins at Big Valley Trail and dead-ends at Norris Lake.
-**Western Section**—A 1.7-mile trail that leads from Big Ridge Dam to Big Valley Trail.

Longer Loop Trails:

The **Big Valley and Dark Hollow West Trail** is a 4.8 mile loop trail. The trailhead is found by taking a right on Big Ridge Park Road from the Gristmill parking lot about 0.2 miles—

Big Valley Trailhead/end:
(36.247512, -83.920536) Moderate. Loop.

You can also follow **Lake Hollow Trail to Ghost Hollow** and then **Dark Hollow Trail**. The trailhead is found by walking left out of the Gristmill parking lot. Moderate. Loop.

Lake Trail Trailhead:
(36.247097, -83.924624)

Big Ridge State Park—
Ghost House Trail
Maynardville, Tennessee
Union County

Ghost House

Ghost House Trail—a haunted place at Big Ridge State Park—

Many years ago, farming families formed small communities that dotted the land now Big Ridge State Park. Then, when the Tennessee Valley Authority built Norris Dam in the early 1930s on the Clinch River, the government forced about ninety-nine families in the vicinity to relocate. They left behind their homes, land, and towns.

Some are now under the waters of Norris Lake or little more than foundations hidden beneath brush and old leaves on the hillsides. But some things remain, including old cemeteries and a few ghosts.

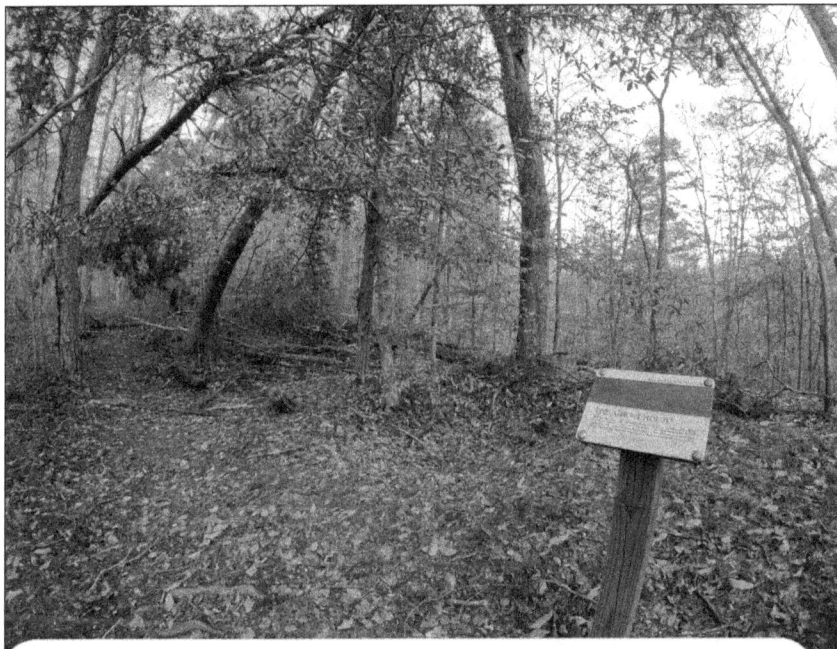

These are the ruins of Ghost House along the trail. I had a strange occurrence here. After hiking to the spot and taking pictures, I strolled around where the old homestead used to be, then started forward to continue my journey to Dark Hollow. As I walked right here, I turned my head a bit to take one last glance, and I saw what I believed to be another hiker, a dark and clear silhouette from the corner of my eye, coming up behind me at a faster pace. I made a quick jog to the left to allow the hiker to pass, but nobody was there when I turned to greet them!

Maston and Martha Hutchinson settled in the area in the 1800s and built a farm there. Their grown daughter, Nancy, contracted tuberculosis and was cared for in the home before she died. During her wake, old-timers would recall that those attending heard a woman crying in the upstairs bedroom where Nancy died. Years later, and after the home was vacated, many refused to travel past the old house for all the eerie sounds that issued from inside.

The Norton Cemetery—

Maston and Martha both died about a month apart in 1910 and are buried in the Norton Cemetery with some of their kin and neighbors. Witnesses have seen those buried within the graveyard rise and stand near their graves.

The Norton Cemetery where the Hutchesons are buried is right along the Ghost House Loop Trail—Martha's grave is front and right behind is Maston's grave.

Parking:
Big Ridge State Park Gristmill and Parking
Big Ridge Park Road
Maynardville, TN 37807
(36.245895, -83.922365)

Ghost House Trail—1.2-miles. Easy to moderate loop trail with options of continuing toward Big Valley and Dark Hollow trails.

The trail begins near the group camp. Next, you will pass **Norton Cemetery**, where the Hutcheson's, the owners of Ghost House, were buried. As you continue, you will head toward the Big Valley Trail and past the remnants of the haunted Hutcheson's Ghost House.

Norton Cemetery
(36.252355, -83.924850)

Ghost House
(36.253959, -83.924229)

Big Ridge State Park—
Indian Rock Loop Trail
Maynardville, Tennessee
Union County

Unsettled Settler

BIG VALLEY TRAIL

Langley Cemetery → 0.2
Indian Rock Loop Trail → 0.4
Ghost House Loop Trail ← 0.7
Big Ridge Park Road ← 1.3

The intersection for Indian Rock Loop Trail—

Sharp's Station, erected in 1784, was a fort built on the slope overlooking the Clinch River that provided settlers in the area protection from Indian attacks where Big Ridge State Park stands today. One of those settlers was 41-year-old Peter Graves. In 1794, Graves was hunting about a quarter-mile from the fort when he heard a turkey gobbling behind some rocks.

As he eased in to locate the birds, he realized too late that the gobbles were not turkeys at all, but several Indians waiting to ambush him. He was quickly overwhelmed, scalped, and murdered. There have been reports of a shadowy figure, bent and limping, trudging near the rocks where the man was killed.

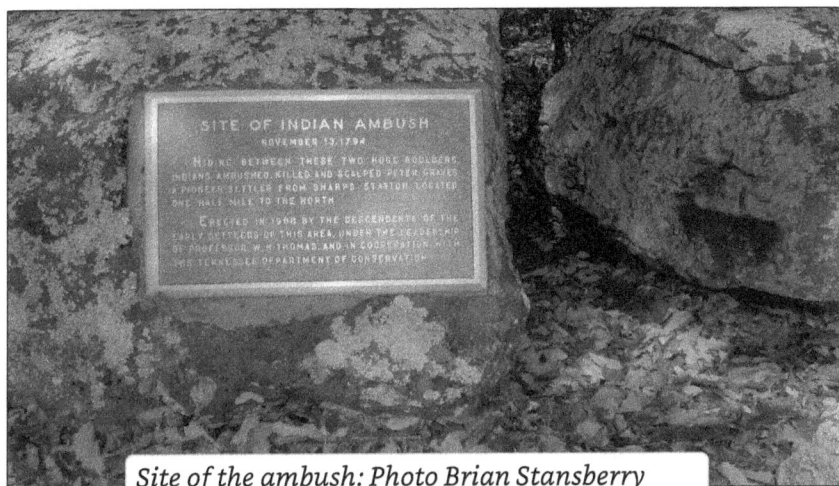

Site of the ambush: Photo Brian Stansberry

 **Parking: Big Ridge State Park Gristmill and Parking**
(36.245895, -83.922365)

 **The Big Valley Trail trailhead** is found by taking a right on Big Ridge Park Road from the Gristmill parking lot about 0.2 miles. (36.247512, -83.920536)

Indian Rock Trail — 2.6 miles. Loop after following primary trail. Very difficult - Experienced hikers only. At some points, it is difficult to make out the trail. Begin at Big Valley Trail and follow Indian Rock Loop Trail. There is a plaque at the location of Peter Graves's murder.

The Smoky Mountains Roaring Forks Motor Nature Trail

The Roaring Fork Motor Nature Trail, named for the Roaring Fork stream running beside the road, is a 6.5 mile heavily trafficked, seasonal point to trail motor path just outside Gatlinburg and within Smoky Mountains National Park. It features pull-offs and parking areas for hiking and viewing genuine historical buildings representing the early mountain region settlements. The motor path, a narrow one-way asphalt road developed from two old roads once running through the community, covers the land that was Spruce Flats. It was a community of about 25 families before it was Smoky Mountain National Park.

It is narrow, steep at some points, and a one-way roadway. It begins at the Noah "Bud" Ogle farmstead, where visitors can take a walking tour of the historic buildings and then hike a short trail of the property. After that, vehicles have the option of continuing the one-way road. Cars and small pickup trucks can seasonally tour the route, and there are parking spaces, trails, and old homesteads to explore inside and out, along with its ghosts and legends.

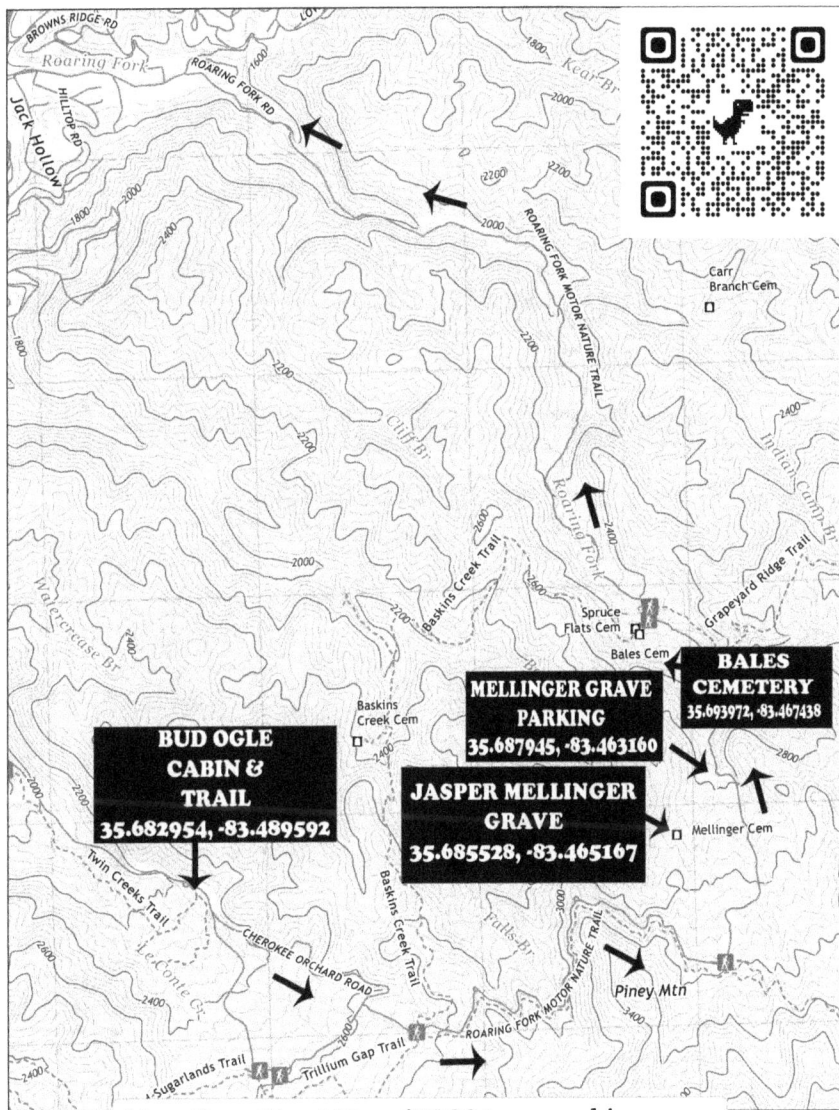

Map: Open Street Maps/USGS topographic maps.

Great Smoky Mountains National Park: Roaring Forks Motor Nature Trail— Bud Ogle Cabin Trail

Gatlinburg, Tennessee
Sevier County

Bud Ogle's Cabin

Noah 'Bud' Ogle Homestead can be found on Cherokee Orchard Road right before the Roaring Fork Motor Nature Trail becomes a one-way. The cabin can be accessed without taking the one-way trail and is not closed seasonally (unless there is bad weather) like the motor trail.

An old, haunted cabin is tucked in the Tennessee mountains just outside a bustling tourist town. The place sits along a small creek just at the edge of a deep pocket of forest. Those who have explored the deserted property when few else are around get a feeling of uneasiness around it. They say it is haunted—

In the early 1800s, settlers arrived in the lands beneath the Smoky Mountains in the southern Appalachian wilderness. They formed small communities in these pockets of forest and farmland like White Oak Flats, now the touristy mountain resort city of Gatlinburg. As the children of these families grew up and married, they set up their own homes not too far away but in more remote areas of White Oak Flats.

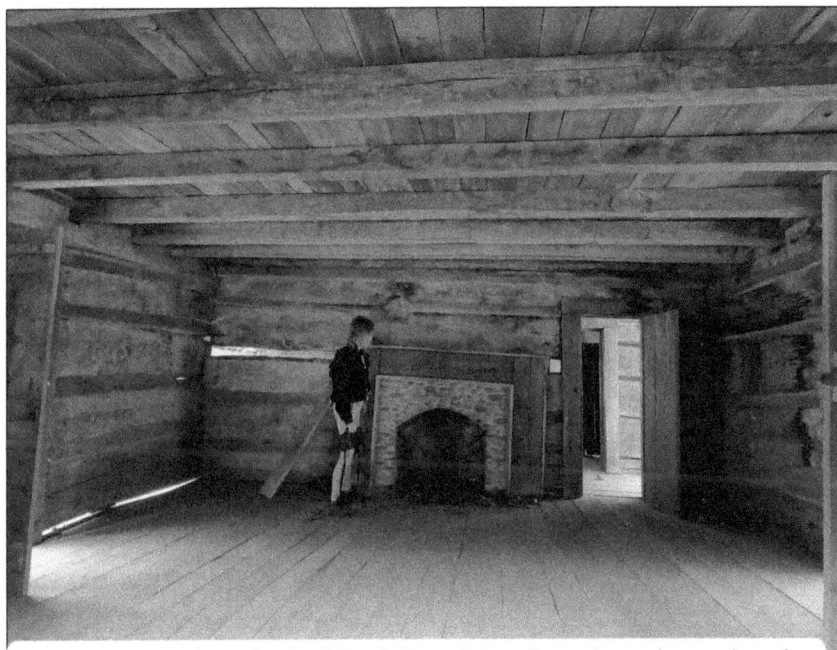

Hikers can explore the inside of the cabin where doors have closed on their own and voices of the dead are heard.

Noah 'Bud' Ogle was among those youngsters of the backcountry; he and his wife Cindy built a cabin and farm along LeConte Creek (formerly known as Mill Creek) in the late 1800s and reared a family. They scratched out a living on the rocky terrain, cultivated crops, and raised animals to survive.

Visitors can explore their old homestead as part of the Great Smoky National Park and it has ghosts from its past.

Occasionally, tourists walking around the old cabin have witnessed doors opening on their own, hear the soft patter of footsteps, and catch the faint sound of voices as if the family who lived there are still going about their daily tasks.

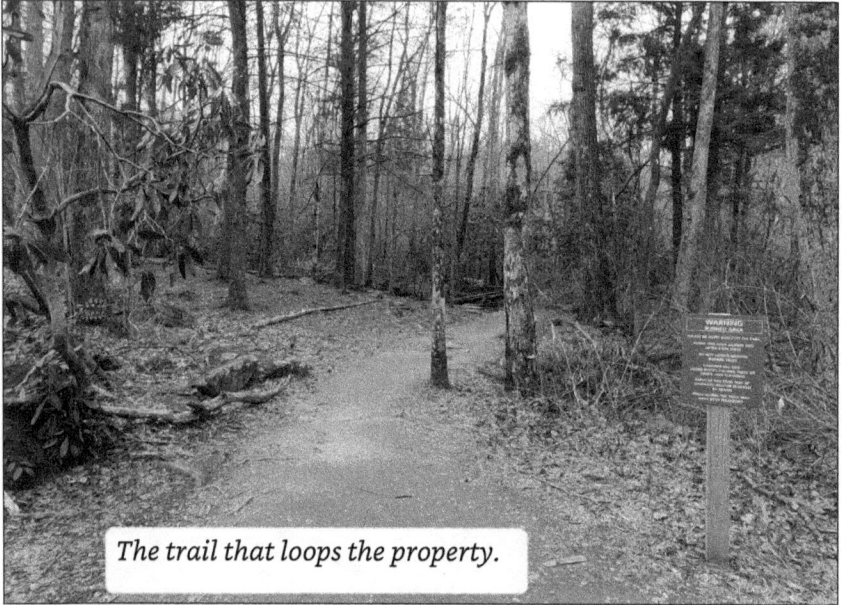

The trail that loops the property.

Noah 'Bud' Ogle Place Nature Trail: 0.8 miles. Loop. Explore inside and outside the home, barn, and property. Noah 'Bud' Ogle Place Nature Trail. Gatlinburg, TN (35.682954, -83.489592)

Hike from Town: If you are walking from town, you can also walk the **Twin Creeks Trail** 2.9 miles (one-way) to the cabin.

Twin Creeks Trail begins: Cherokee Orchard Road, Gatlinburg, TN (35.700572, -83.511111)

Great Smoky Mountains National Park: Roaring Forks Motor Nature Trail— Mellinger Cemetery Trail
Gatlinburg, Tennessee
Sevier County

The Vanishing of Jasper Mellinger

Old cabins in the community of Spruce Flats—

The nearby hamlet of Roaring Fork, called Spruce Flats, was also settled this way along a hollow that heads beneath Mount LeConte and ends near Gatlinburg. Spruce Flats had its own school, church, mill, and general store. Among those who lived in the community were the Bales, Reagans, Ogles, Clabos, and Mellingers. The latter family would be long remembered for a mysterious disappearance, and many believe an unsolved murder.

Jasper and Martha Mellinger lived on a 30-acre homestead along the Roaring Fork in a two-room cabin with a vegetable garden, a small field for growing corn, and a barn and pasture for livestock. A farmer by livelihood, Jasper was also a blacksmith, which provided extra income for essentials he could not barter with others living in the valley beneath the mountains. It was a hardscrabble life for the family, but the couple, along with their children, Lutrisha, age 18, and Edward, age 23, always got by.

The area the Mellingers once lived.

That is, until the harsh dead of winter of 1901. There was no work to be found close to home when, one morning, Martha watched her husband leave the homestead searching for a job. Jasper was 64 years old when he set out toward Hazel Creek in North Carolina, a distance as the crow flies of about twenty-four miles, and the location of several copper mine camps. He knew the folks in the mining areas could use his skills as a blacksmith there, and he and Martha were becoming quite desperate for extra cash.

The trails, creek paths, and crude roads he would take in the undeveloped backcountry were raggedy and overgrown as many were mostly traveled by deer and bears. They were certainly not of the standard rural streets and cleanly maintained hiking trails that we see today. Instead, Jasper would have to ascend steep and rubble-ridden mountains, then descend on the other side, always wary his next step might be off a cliff with an edge concealed by thick brush. But he felt no need to worry; the blacksmith was a man of the mountains and familiar with the unforgiving terrain.

His trip might last a week or more, and Martha certainly did not expect word of her husband's movements along the way. News traveled slowly in the mountains, and few passersby would have crossed paths with him then taken the time to walk to her remote home to offer an update. She also had not gotten any premonitions or forewarnings, leading her to believe something was amiss. No dog had howled at night to foreshadow a death, nor had her ears rang to mimic the church bell that would toll out if someone in her family passed away. And as she could recall, no bird had flown too close to home because that was a big sign of death she had heard passed down in her family. Many years earlier, that had happened to Richard Reagan, who owned the town mill and blacksmith shop in White Oak Flats. One day in 1829, while he was sitting on the porch smoking a pipe, a little bird alit on his head. He leaped from his seat and declared it was a "death sign." A few days later, Richard died of a fractured skull after a limb hit him in the head when he was taking horses from the pasture to the barn.

All superstitions aside, when Jasper did not return and weeks turned to months, she began to fret. A search party was sent to find the missing man and the only word she received was that her husband had spent his first night with the Ownby family in Elkmont by the Sugarland Mountains.

He was warmly greeted as their guest with a bed at night and breakfast in the morning before he went on his way. That was the last anyone recalled seeing Jasper Mellinger. They traced his steps to a spur of Cold Knob near Miry Ridge before any sign of the man vanished.

Then, four years after Jasper disappeared, a young man of Wear's Valley was dying and thought he should rid his conscience of a horrible deed. Years before, he and his father, John Beasley, were setting bear traps in the middle of a trail without warning signs which was illegal. When they returned to check on them, they found a man with his leg caught in the bear trap, dead from exposure and starvation. Fearing they would be jailed, the father demanded the son keep the secret of the death to himself. Instead, they covered the corpse with hemlock branches and left the body to rot.

Looking in the direction of the place called "Mellinger Death Ridge," named for the man who lost his life there and the unforgiving terrain Jasper traveled to find work.

Upon hearing the news, Ownby family members with whom Jasper Mellinger had spent the night on his journey went out searching around Cold Knob, where the dying man described he and his father had left the dead traveler.

As they came across a pool of water frequented by wild game, they discovered a pocket watch, three dollars in coins, and a rifle with JM carved into the stock. Then they came upon the scattering of human bones.

The man who had set the bear trap was arrested and tried but released because of insufficient evidence. Some say the dying young man did not give the whole truth; Jasper Mellinger was still alive when the two trappers came upon him, and they murdered him with a club to the head. Still, others say Jasper was just unlucky that day; he fell and died by no man's hand. That answer, we will never know.

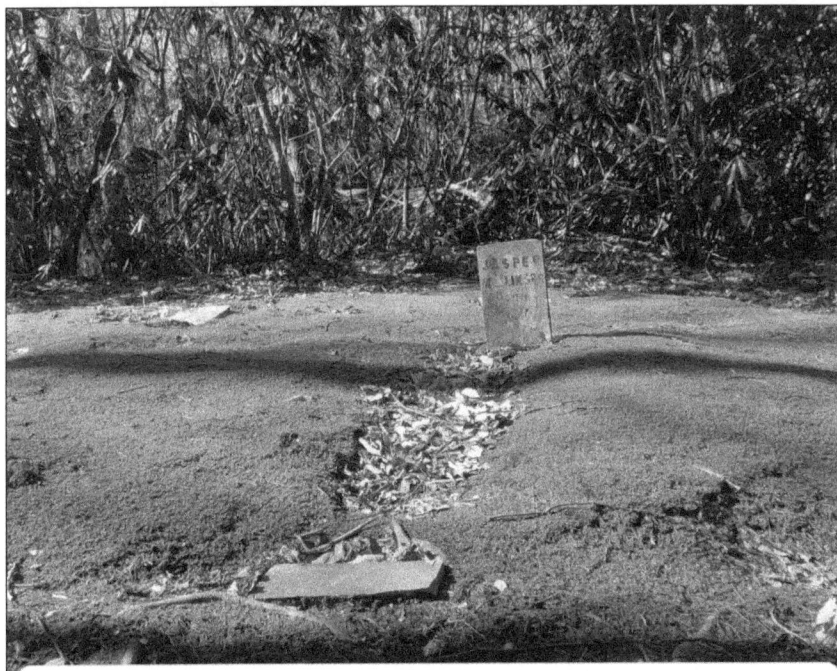

Jasper Mellinger's grave on a lonely, steep ridgetop along the Roaring Fork Motor Trail. The trail to it is not as clearly defined and on a steep climb, but worth the short hike.

Martha lost her eyesight and moved to the Poor House, where she lived for nearly 20 years, seemingly happy and cherished by the staff and residents. The ridge where Jasper Mellinger's life ended is called "Mellinger Death Ridge."

Jasper's body was brought home and buried in a cemetery on a knoll beneath Round Top Mountain near his old homestead. Two of his children, who died in the 1870s during diphtheria outbreaks, are buried nearby. Nowadays, hikers can take the unmaintained trail and gaze down upon the sunken grave of Jasper Mellinger covered in soft green moss, and reflect upon the mystery and legend still surrounding his disappearance.

Mellinger Cemetery—

Parking: Roaring Forks Nature Trail #8
(35.687945, -83.463160)

Mellinger Grave

Jasper Mellinger Grave Trail: (35.688082, -83.463263)

Marker #8. You will cross the bridge over Rocky Spur Branch stream and the parking lot is directly after on the left (*Look for a wooden sign on the right with 8 on it*). Take the short walk back to the bridge and right before it, there is a trail to the right. Hike about 0.5 miles one-way. The first part of the hike is flat. After, there is a really steep climb to the top of the ridge to the graveyard. Out and back. Rugged.

Jasper Mellinger Grave: (35.685528, -83.465167)

Great Smoky Mountains National Park: Roaring Forks Motor Nature Trail—Grapeyard Ridge Trail to Bales Cemetery
Gatlinburg, Tennessee
Sevier County

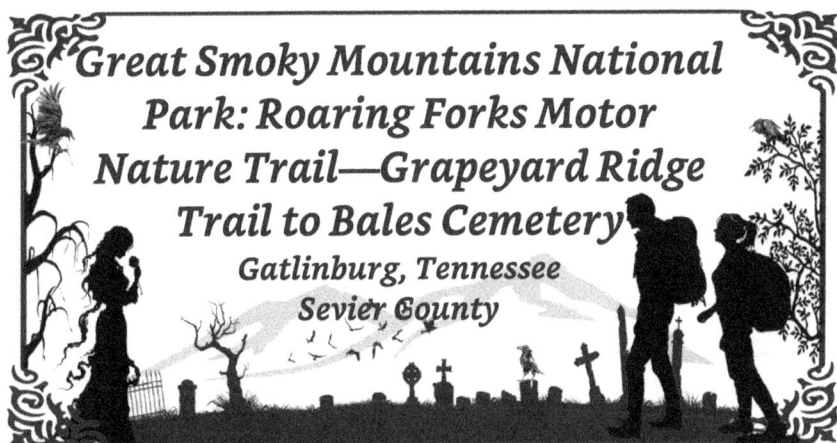

The Peculiar Grave of Giles Reagan

The Reagan Homestead—

Among the early families in this area of Roaring Fork was Alfred Reagan, who farmed the rock-strewn valley. He was the community's jack-of-all-trades, owning a gristmill and store and offered blacksmithing on the side. He was also a carpenter and provided coffins for those in the community who died.

Alfred had a son named Giles. In the 1920s, Alfred sold some timber to Andy Huff, who cut and milled the wood. While working at the mill, Giles lost his leg in an accident, and although he lived, he insisted on burying his leg in a cemetery marked with a stone and given the proper funeral rites from a local preacher. However, years later, when he died, the rest of Giles was buried in the old cemetery in Gatlinburg.

Bales Cemetery and trail—

You can stop and take the short trail to Bale's Cemetery along the Grapeyard Ridge Trail, walk through the old boneyard, and try to guess which stone was laid for Giles Reagan's leg!

Parking: Roaring Fork Motor Tour Parking #7 Grapeyard Ridge Trailhead (Along Baskins Creek Trail) (35.694280, -83.466592)

Trail: Bales Cemetery
In and out. Maintained trail.
(35.693972, -83.467438)

Great Smoky Mountains National Park: Roaring Forks Motor Nature Trail—Roaring Forks Road

Gatlinburg, Tennessee
Sevier County

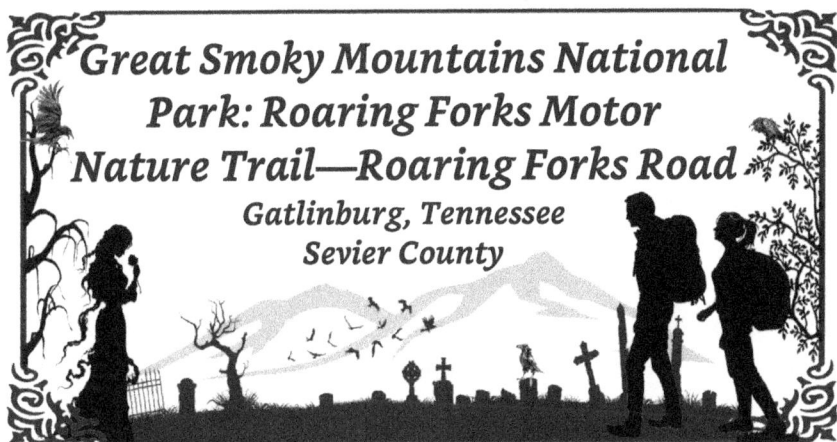

Hitchhiking Lucy of Roaring Forks

An old cabin nearly hidden across from Roaring Forks in the area of an old ghost story—

On a chilly autumn night in the early 1900s, a young man named Foster was traveling by horseback from Gatlinburg and toward his modest cabin in the mountains. It was dark except for the shine of a full moon mostly lighting his path. Occasionally, clouds crossed the sky and cast shadows on the rutted road leaving all sorts of ghastly imaginations like thieves and spooks playing in his mind.

He decided to keep to an old country road that made its way along the Roaring Fork stream and through the quiet community of Spruce Flats. It was comforting to pass a house with warm candlelight bobbing inside a window or catch the faint scent of chimney smoke from time to time.

He would not be out on such a cold night, except that his journey had been very important even though it had not been as successful as he had hoped. Foster was heading home from a late church meeting. Now he was not overly religious as folks go, but as he and other young men knew, lots of mamas and daddies and their daughters attended these gatherings. It was the closest thing to a social event that anyone knew to meet nice girls. Moreover, Foster was of marriageable age; he grasped it was time to find a wife.

The haunted road—

As he rode in silence, he sniffed the air. It smelled sweet like that of an oncoming snow—and curiously, too, it had a hint of the bitter pong of burnt wood. Then as he made his way beside the stream, suddenly before him, a girl appeared.

Startled, Foster gasped. He noted straight away that she was barefoot and dressed in nothing but a plain, white muslin gown—the style women wore when they went to bed. Had she gone outside to perform some task she had forgotten before bedtime and gotten turned around in the dark of night? He was not sure if he should avert his eyes as she approached; he had never seen a stranger, a woman in her underclothes. Yet her beauty so enthralled Foster, he could do no more than pull back the rope reins in his fingers, bring his horse to a halt, and stare with mouth agape at the figure before him. She, too, stopped and looked up into his eyes with a questioning gaze.

Foster cleared his throat and mumbled something unintelligible before he gained the nerve to stumble through, "Can I offer you a ride? Surely you are frozen out here." She did not answer aloud but slowly bobbed her head up and down and extended her hand upward toward Foster. A brisk wind whistled through, and the clouds swept past. Foster hurriedly leaned over and snatched up her fingers. He could not help but notice that her hands were very warm to the touch, and her hair still had the deep scent of chimney smoke. Surely her home was within sight as she could not have ventured far. After he helped her onto the saddle in front of him, her bare arm rose. The girl's fingers pointed along the road beside Roaring Fork.

Such, they traveled for quite some time and, of course, in silence. Yet as the young woman leaned lazily back into his chest, he felt her warmth, and it made him feel a bit smitten with her. So, he grinned to himself for finding such a catch and decided if he could get the nerve up, he would ask her if he could come for a visit one day. Foster, however, never got to inquire. Darkness came upon them, and the moon slipped away with a sudden gust smelling of a looming storm.

Unexpectedly, the girl snatched the reins, halted the horse, and slipped off the saddle and to the earth below. She bolted into the woods, but only moments before she did, she looked up longingly at Foster with a tear running from one eye.

Along Roaring Forks Motor Trail—

Foster tarried there as long as he could, but the wind and a hint of sleet began to pelt his cheeks. He sniffed the breeze sure he smelt a lingering bit of woodsmoke. He thought it might have come from the girl, but hoped it drifted down from a cabin with a warm fire awaiting her. He made a thorough search of the area, but in the blackness of the oncoming early winter storm, he knew he must leave. Surely, the girl knew her way from here.

Foster returned to his home safely and waited out the storm, but the woman was on his mind every moment. He knew as soon as the road was passable, he would return to the place of the mysterious hitchhiker. So, he did. Foster followed the narrow road along the Roaring Forks, past the place he had picked her up and then upon locating the point where the girl had dismounted, he discovered a tiny worn path that weaved its way into the woods. He followed it and came upon a little cabin—one that looked fairly new.

Anxiously, Foster walked a stone pathway and then across a porch. He stood before the door, raised his hand, and rapped his knuckles on the wood. His heart beat wildly; so many nights, he had tossed and turned, dreaming of this moment when he would meet the pretty young woman again.

Before he could drop his arm, the door opened. But it was not a young woman peering out at him, and instead, stood an old man and woman.

"I am looking for a girl I offered a ride to recently," he mumbled. "I . . ." But before he could finish, the man held up a hand to stop Foster's words.

"That would be our daughter Lucy," he said softly, and Foster's heart jumped, even though he saw the sad turn to the man's eyes. "You are not the only one with whom she has sought a ride. But she is dead and has been for ten years. You see, she was killed when our cabin along the creek burned down. We could not bear to live at the location our only child lost her life, so we rebuilt up the Roaring Creek a bit. Now, when she sees riders pass, she sometimes flags them down in search of us—"

There have been others who have picked up the hitchhiking ghost of Lucy. Perhaps as you drive the Roaring Creek Motor Trail, you will have a young woman flag you down. It is your choice to pick her up or not!

The Smoky Mountains Cades Cove

Cades Cove was settled in the early 1800s, a farming community beneath Thunderhead Mountain and resting in a mountain basin. It grew and endured with three churches, a gristmill, farms, orchards, and homesteads until the late 1920s, when the government forced the landowners to sell their property or sign life leases so a national park could be built.

It is now an 11-mile, one-way motor trail with stops so visitors can hike trails and tour the remaining historic buildings, once the beloved homes and farms of Cades Cove landowners. In addition, there are numerous hiking trails, including a five-mile loop trail, where hikers may bump into the ghostly inhabitants of the settlement's past.

The road is open to motor vehicles from sunrise until sunset daily, weather permitting—excluding Wednesdays all day from early May through late September when only bicycle and foot traffic are allowed. Seasonally, expect the traffic to be bumper to bumper.

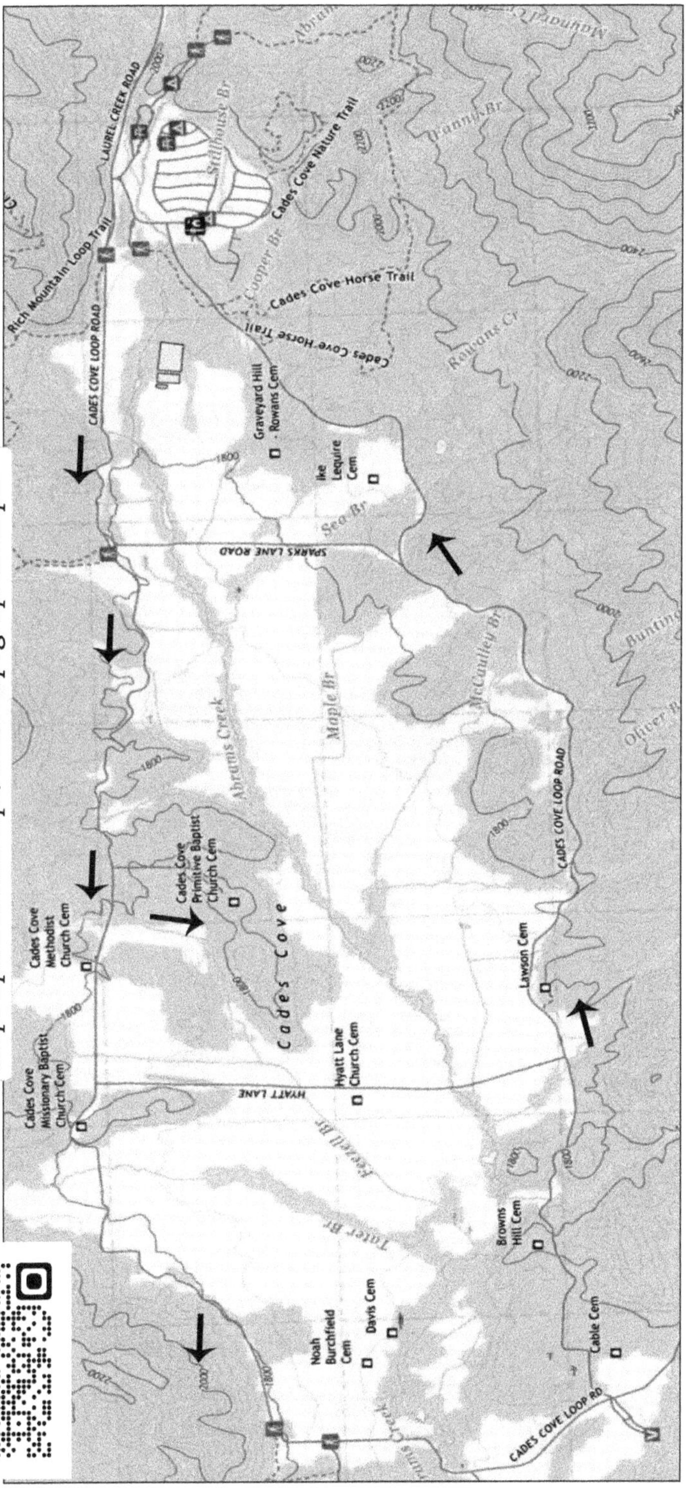

Map: Open Street Maps/USGS topographic maps.

LAUREL CREEK ROAD

Abra...

Stillhouse Br

Manua...

Cades Cove Nature Trail

Rich Mountain Loop Trail

Cooper Br

Cades Cove-Horse Trail

CADES COVE LOOP ROAD

Cades Cove Horse Trail

Rabbit... Cr

Graveyard Hill

Rowans Cem

Ike Lequire Cem

Sea Br

SPARKS LANE ROAD

McCauley Br

Bunting...

Oliver B

Abrams Creek

Maple Br

CADES COVE LOOP ROAD

Cades Cove Primitive Baptist Church Cem

Cades Cove Methodist Church Cem

Cades Cove

Lawson Cem

Cades Cove Missionary Baptist Church Cem

Hyatt Lane Church Cem

HYATT LANE

Feezell Br

Tater Br

Browns Hill Cem

Noah Burchfield Cem

Davis Cem

Cable Cem

CADES COVE LOOP RD

Great Smoky Mountains National Park: Cades Cove— Cades Cove Loop Road
Gatlinburg, Tennessee
Sevier County

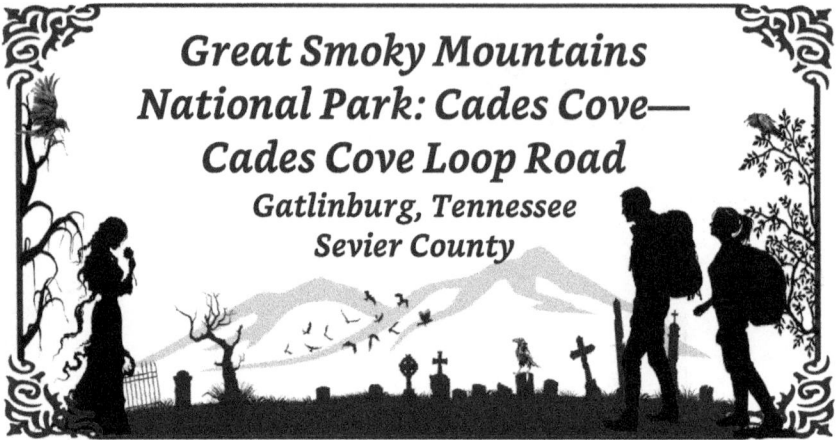

The Cussing Cover—Folklore from the Cove

Whistling Branch, the stream in Cades Cove where one of the Smoky Mountain's most treasured folktales took root—

Long ago, Mavis and Basil Estep made their home in a two-room cabin in the heart of Cades Cove along the stream of Whistling Branch. The pair were content with each other as couples tend to be; they looked after each other's needs, nurtured their children, and (mostly over Mavis' irritation when Basil cussed over some trifle aggravation) bickered back and forth occasionally.

They followed the Good Book to protect their souls, paid attention to nature to harvest their crops, and respected the traditional beliefs passed down to them from their elders. It was the final, the folklore, that provided persistent worry to one member of the family. Not all lore, as such. She was not crazy. But when Mavis was born, it was during a wild thunderstorm. And since she was old enough to remember, people would often remind her that babes, like herself, born during such a gale, would find their death by a lightning strike. The tale was so ingrained in her mind that Mavis had an overwhelming fear of storms.

Every morning after getting out of bed, she would peer out the door, seeing if the sky had a reddish hue because, as the saying goes, "Red Sky in the morning, sailor take warning. Red sky at night is a sailor's delight." So great was her fear that if the sky was even a pale pink, she would not step past the threshold of the front door. If a dark cloud passed over the sky when she was in her garden, she would grab up her skirts to her shins and race frantically for the safety of her house. When inside, she refused to pick up her patchwork quilt-making needles because some dear aunt had divulged that the metal from the needles would attract lightning. And she most certainly refused to allow metal beds in the home in case lightning came through the window and struck the frame!

On sunny days, Mavis was able to tuck away her fears, and when her tasks were complete, she would pull out square scraps of fabric cut from old clothing and blankets and the occasional piece of store-bought cloth. Then, she would lay them all out in a pretty pattern and sew them together in a patchwork quilt. Not only did Mavis adore making quilts (and she made a lot of them), but she was also well-known in the Cades Cove community for her skills.

There were quilts in the open room, quilts in the bedrooms, and quilts tacked over the windows and doors to keep the cold and bugs out. There were quilts on the beds and inside trunks, and one even donned the kitchen table. But of all the quilts that Mavis had made, one was particularly special to her. It was the comforter she fondly called the "Cussing Cover," for when she made it, she had used a well-worn red flannel shirt belonging to Basil, and it was the very one he had been wearing during their first marital spat which Basil had cussed up a storm.

Cades Cove Motor Trail, left—

Mavis Estep died, and lightning did not kill her. It was a sickness that took her life. When she knew her time was due, her dying words to her husband of so many years was askance of a promise that he would not sell her treasured quilts nor bring a metal bed into the house and place them on the bed. With his solemn nod of head in agreement, Mavis passed away quite contently. Mavis was in the grave nearly a year before Basil found a pretty young wife named Trulie Jane Lawson and brought her to his cabin. Trulie Jane was a big woman, much taller and much wider than Mavis.

She was tall enough and wide enough that the bed she and Basil shared was far too small for her frame. Right away, the young wife made it clear that the small wooden bed in their room would simply not be suitable. She tossed and turned and almost fell out, and with every toss and turn, it creaked and groaned and kept the two awake. Nothing would make her happy unless she had a newfangled metal bed.

A cabin along the trail—

Basil thought about it long and hard. He scratched his head, thinking about Mavis' deathbed wishes. But she was long-dead and buried seven feet down. It was not as if his first wife could make his life difficult if he got one of those new metal beds. Trulie Jane was very much alive. And she could very much inconvenience him greatly should he deny her wishes. Such, when his new wife insisted, Basil bought a metal bed and moved it into their house.

All was fine until one cool evening in the fall. Trulie Jane awakened during the night feeling chilled and strode to the cupboard where the family stored the blankets and quilts.

One pretty red patchwork quilt caught her eye, and she wiggled it out from the layers of other quilts. It was so colorful and perfect! Basil had never told her the story of the Cussing Cover or the deathbed promise to Mavis. He was sound asleep when the woman returned, so he did not have the chance to stop Trulie Jane when she tucked herself cozily into bed with the Cussing Cover overtop them, closed her eyes, and went back to sleep. It was not long before something awakened Trulie Jane, and she peeked out from beneath her cover. Lo and behold, the ghost of Mavis Estep was floating at the foot of the bed, cursing and yowling. Trulie Jane began to scream, and Basil was startled out of his sleep. But by the time he could focus on the foot of the bed, the ghost was gone.

Basil convinced his new wife that she had a nightmare because he had not heard or seen anything. Finally, after some time, they fell to sleep again. A couple of hours later, a brilliant ball of light burst into the room and sent Trulie Jane flying across the floor. As she stood and looked to where her bed had been, there was nothing but the charred corpse of Basil Estep. All else in the home was untouched. When she told those in the community about the lightning bolt that killed her husband, nobody could recall a storm passing through the valley that night.

Trulie Jane refused to keep any of Mavis' quilts after that, giving them away to the Estep's daughters. In turn, they sold the quilts to local stores over time. Those locals who knew the Cussing Cover story stayed far away from those quilts, and if you are in a shop, you may hear one ask if looking at hand-sewn quilts, from whom the cover came. And it is probably in your best interest, should you be looking, to ask the same!

The **Primitive Baptist Church** in Cades Cove was established in 1827. The building located there now was erected about 60 years later. Years ago, while touring the cabin, a family caught pictures of a ghostly woman coming through the wall. Others have seen orbs of bright lights floating above the graves in the cemetery. You can visit the church by making the first turnoff along the Cades Cove Loop Road after the John Oliver Cabin.

Motor Trail: 11 miles. Drive or seasonally, hike or bike, on Wednesdays. Loop. Within, there are many trails to take where you can tour old cabins and barns and might run into the long-dead of this ghost town community including:

Abrams Falls Trailhead and Parking just off Cades Cove motor loop: Moderately difficult. Loop. 2.5 miles (one-way) Abrams Falls Trail
Townsend, TN 37882
(35.591439, -83.852572)

The Smoky Mountains
Elkmont

Elkmont, a onetime logging community and resort destination, can now be explored as the National Park Service continues restoring the buildings and maintaining outlying roads as trails. But those entering the almost-abandoned town should know that some of those who once lived or vacationed here do not want to leave—even after death.

Great Smoky Mountains National Park: Elkmont Daisy Town/Jakes Creek Trail/ Elkmont Nature Trail
Elkmont/Gatlinburg, Tennessee
Sevier County

Ghost Town Ghosts

The town of Elkmont around 1918 (Courtesy of Great Smoky Mountains NP archives)—You will drive right through the heart of Elkmont near the ruins of the Wonderland Hotel here: (35.663093, -83.590149) and through the Elkmont Campground Roads A and B (35.659037, -83.581340).

Early pioneers settled the area called Little River in the 1830s where Jake's Creek and the Little River come together.

Then, it was not much more than a small community of homesteaders dotting the landscape. However, it was not until the early 1900s that it received its current name of Elkmont when it became the base for the booming Little River Lumber Company that clear-cut its way through the Smoky Mountains. The company built the Little River Railroad to transport the harvested logs dragged down the mountains by horses, mules, and oxen.

The Wonderland Club Hotel in 1921 (Courtesy of Great Smoky Mountains NP archives). No longer there—

The lumber company workers and their families lived in homes that were rented from the lumber company, purchased their food and supplies from the company-owned store, and the loggers worked long hours, six days a week. In 1911, the company built a hotel, Wonderland Hotel, another lucrative business. In addition, they added an observation car to the logging train to transport vacationers from larger cities like Knoxville, a two-and-a-half-hour ride, to the hotel. Over the years, the Little River Lumber Company sold strips of land for a private social club. Several resort communities sprouted up after as popular vacation destinations like one called Daisy Town for those wishing to get away from the heat and pollution of the city in summer.

As this type of vacation declined in the late 1900s, the resort and Elkmont fell to ghost town ruins. However, Daisy Town, now renovated by the National Park Service, is one of the areas that hikers can visit along with trails featuring traces of a logging and resort past. Occasionally along the old trails and in the buildings, visitors see ghostly remnants, too, of its past.

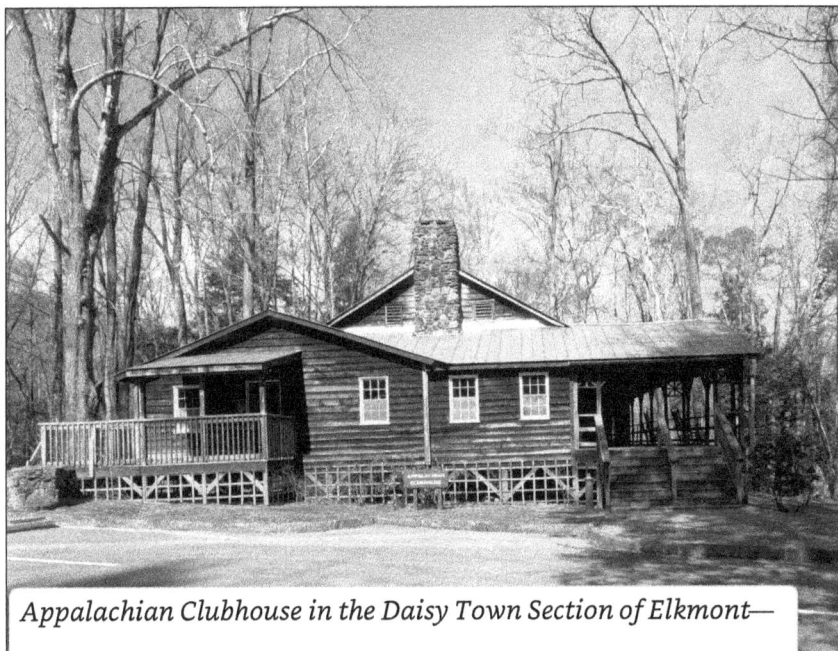

Appalachian Clubhouse in the Daisy Town Section of Elkmont—

The Appalachian Club was a hub for socializing among the vacationers and hosted parties and dances with live music. You can hike to it along the roadway after passing through Daisy Town. People from its bygone years haunt the town—one of the park workers was cleaning the clubhouse after an event when he observed an elderly man in the older part of the building. As he moved forward to address the gentleman and tell him that this part of the Clubhouse was off-limits, the old man vanished! He later learned that it was a man who had drowned in Jake's Creek in 1914.

The park service built the Campgrounds and facilities on the old logging town and CCC campsite. Occasionally passersby within the grounds are startled by the sight of a logger ambling past before he vanishes. On June 30th, 1909, a train stacked high with logs traveling from Elkmont hit a sharp curve on a rainy day and overturned. Although no passengers died, engineer Eugene A "Daddy" Bryson and brakeman Charles Jenkins were killed. Some believe that it is these men who have been seen strolling near the Little River Trail.

Elkmont Nature Trail—where I heard ghostly singing—

While hiking along the Elkmont Nature Trail, I continually heard a distinct female voice singing brashly and loudly at the top of her lungs, almost as if she was that one overly devout woman who belts out the church hymn louder than anybody else during the Sunday morning service. (Oh, and please do not judge me on that one. I am a preacher's daughter. Anybody who attends church regularly knows someone that over sings everyone else—) Regardless, it was a cool winter day and there was no one nearby.

I eased along the trail trying to make out the song and see if perhaps there was just some very happy hiker ahead of me. When I finally was able to get into a position above where I could see where the singing was coming from, there was absolutely nobody there. Was it a ghostly remnant of Elkmont's logging past or a hiker's voice picked up with the wind? I cannot be certain. But when I looked on an old map of the town, I could see there was a church across the road and not far from the trail at one time. Perhaps others taking the pretty walk will hear the singing and validate my experience!

You can visit the Cabin of Levi Trentham, bear trapper and guide, who became the legendary "Prophet of The Smokies" for the telling of visions he would see and came to pass. According to locals and guests in the cottages, this man with a long beard was quite a character. Levi Trentham home.

Image of Levi Trentham— (Courtesy of Great Smoky Mountains NP archives)

Wonderland Hotel Ruins- Elkmont Club Buildings
(35.662877, -83.589016)
Parking: There are designated pull-offs nearby

Parking: For both Daisy Town and Jakes Creek Trailhead:
(35.652606, -83.581683)

Daisy Town—The Appalachian Clubhouse is located at the end of the street—

Trail 1: Hike to and through homes at **Daisy Town** abandoned ghost town. Then continue along Jakes Creek Trail.

Trail 2: Jakes Creek Trail—Continue through Daisy town and along an old roadbed. 3.3 miles (one-way) Easy. Ruins of old homes and an actual cabin, Avent Cabin (about 2.7 miles), along the route to explore.
Jakes Creek Trail Trailhead Out and Back.
(35.651897, -83.581144)

Trail 3: Little River Trail: Explore the structures known as Millionaire's Row. Easy hike along an old logging road. Round trip: 4.9 miles. Out and back.
Trail and Parking: Near Elkmont Campground) (35.653532, -83.579456)

Trail 4: Elkmont Nature Trail through areas where houses once stood and directly across from the town proper. Elkmont Nature Trail: Loop. Easy.
(35.657787, -83.580468)

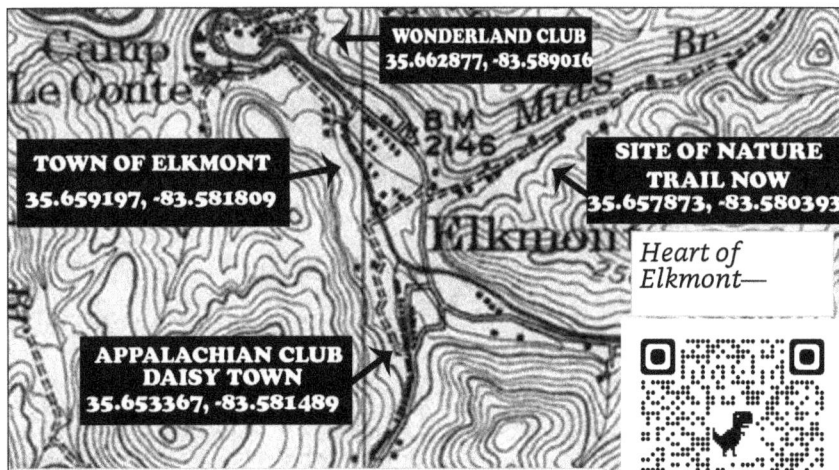

WONDERLAND CLUB
35.662877, -83.589016

TOWN OF ELKMONT
35.659197, -83.581809

SITE OF NATURE
TRAIL NOW
35.657873, -83.580393

Heart of Elkmont—

APPALACHIAN CLUB
DAISY TOWN
35.653367, -83.581489

Map circa 1933 showing the layout of the buildings/homes (small squares). Map: USGS

North Carolina

Great Smoky Mountains National Park: Noland Creek Trail
Bryson City, North Carolina
Swain County

Legends of
Spearfinger & the Dancing Lights

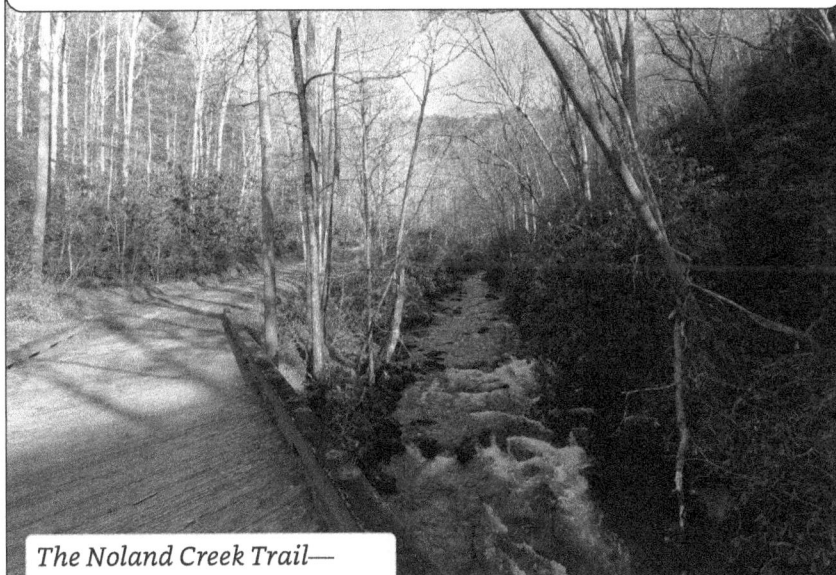

The Noland Creek Trail—

Many years ago, in the heads of streams nearly hidden beneath the shadows of dense forest and amongst dark passes and ridges in the Smoky Mountains, there was a horrible ogress. The Cherokee called her "U'tlun'ta," One With Pointed Spear or Spearfinger. She had power over stone and could strike it together to make bridges that she traversed from one place to another.

She could take the shape of anything she liked to serve whatever purpose she had in mind. And that purpose, it was always ghastly. In her human form, she looked like a harmless old woman. Yet, harmless, she was not. Her entire body was covered in stone-like skin, and no weapon could pierce through the tough hide. The forefinger of her right hand was long and as skinny as a sharp knife, which she used to stab anyone with whom she came into contact.

Her favorite prey were young children. If she heard them playing outside their camp, she would take the form of an old woman and follow their sweet scent, hobbling as if she was having great difficulty walking. "I am tired," she would say and sit down beside them as if wanting to watch them play. Then with her speared-finger hand hidden in her dress, she would call out to one of them. "Come sit on grandma's lap, and I will sing you a song and play with your hair." And any one of them would come skipping and prancing over and plop their little head happily on her lap in anticipation of the special attention. U'tlun'ta crooned and cooed over the child and slipped her fingers through its hair until the child fell into a blissful nap. It was then that U'tlun'ta whipped her hand from its hidden pocket in her clothing, sinking the speared forefinger through the tender flesh of the back of the child's neck until she felt the tip pierce the liver. Then, the liver, she would drag out and eat it as it dripped with blood, smacking her lips and sighing contentedly to herself while the other children ran screeching away.

There were times that U'tlun'ta would walk into a camp and wait until a man or woman was alone and spear them with her finger. She could do so without killing them, and when she did, the person's health would wane over the course of days until they eventually died. Only then did they recognize that U'tlun'ta had been among them.

The Cherokee tired of U'tlun'ta's sport. They waited for her to come to camp in her old woman form so they could kill her. They dug a hole for her feeble legs to fall into and knew she was so heavy that she could not climb out. They waited and the spear-fingered woman came upon the trail and stumbled into the hole. The warriors rushed in and fought long and hard, but her skin was stone, and their arrows and knives would not penetrate. Finally, a little titmouse flew down, landing above her ribcage. "Here! Here! Here!" It called out. "Here! Here! Here!" The men believed it was a sign that her chest must be U'tlun'ta's most vulnerable part of her body and began to aim their arrows there, but to no avail. In anger, one warrior caught the little titmouse and cut off its tongue for lying. Not long after, a chickadee flitted down from a tree and landed on her right hand. "Hit here, here, here!" It cried. Not wanting to fall prey to another deceitful bird, the warriors did not want to waste their arrows again. But they had no choice as the ogress began to climb from the hole. They listened to the chickadee and aimed their arrows where the bird had perched and the spear-fingered hand she held in a tight fist. Many arrows fell there, and one finally hit where the spear joined her palm and the place her cold heart lay. And she died.

Not all believe she is gone. Mysterious and eerie shrieks come from the mountains where U'tlun'ta once lurked near the dark and tree-covered old roadbed that is the Noland Creek Trail. But the Spearfinger ogress, perhaps passing you in the form of another hiker, is not the only mysterious being you might run into on the trail. Strange floating lights have appeared in front of those who have gotten lost walking off its path. When hikers follow them, the little orbs lead them to safety. Once there were homesteads along this path. Most believe the odd lights are those of a settler. When searching for his lost daughter, he was killed by Indians.

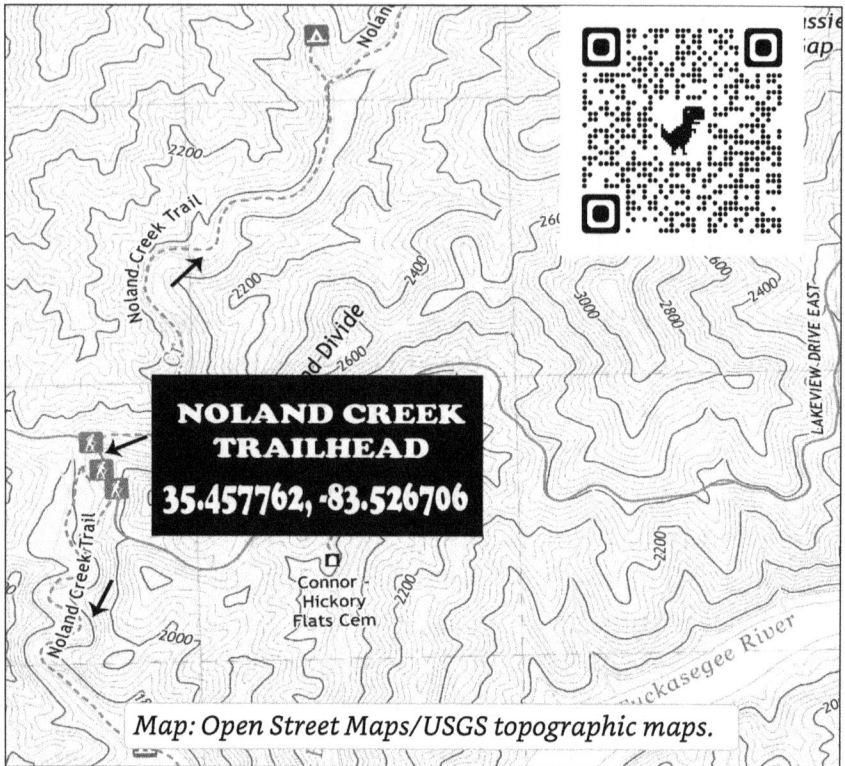

Map: Open Street Maps/USGS topographic maps.

Parking: Lakeview Drive East Parking #2
(35.457311, -83.526560)

Trail: Noland Creek Trailhead: Just a short hike at the end of the guardrail. (35.457762, -83.526706)

Trail 1: Noland Creek Trail South: When you reach the bottom of the trailhead access, there is a sign showing you can go left to hike the 1.0 miles one-way to Fontana Lake. Out and back. Easy.

Trail 2: Noland Creek Trail North: Go right. Heads through a historically populated area with home ruins and cemeteries (an estimated 200 graveyards). You can hike well over 8.0 miles (one-way) with backcountry camps along the way. Out and back. Moderate.

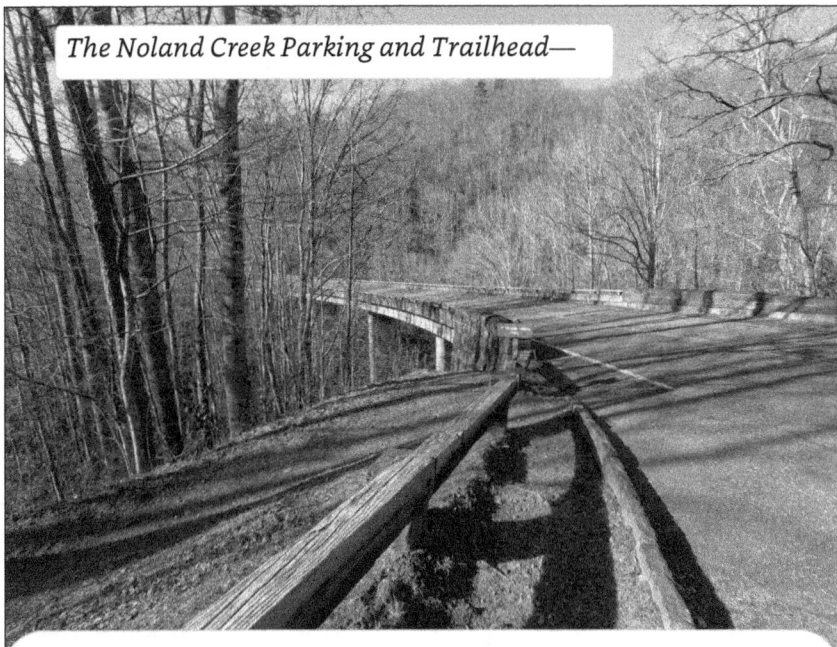

The Noland Creek Parking and Trailhead—

For those whose curiosity is piqued by the abandoned: If you continue on Lakeview Drive 0.7 miles, it will come to a stop not far from a tunnel, called the **Road to Nowhere Tunnel**. (35.459418, -83.538014). When Fontana Dam was built and residents were forced to leave, the government agreed to provide access to the cemeteries and ancestral lands of the community. However, the road was never completed due to environmental issues, hence the signs you may see on your way through town, "Road to Nowhere—A Broken Promise—" You can walk through the tunnel and hike a 3.2-mile loop Gold Mine Trail. (From parking lot to tunnel is rough asphalt and accessible by most wheelchairs.)

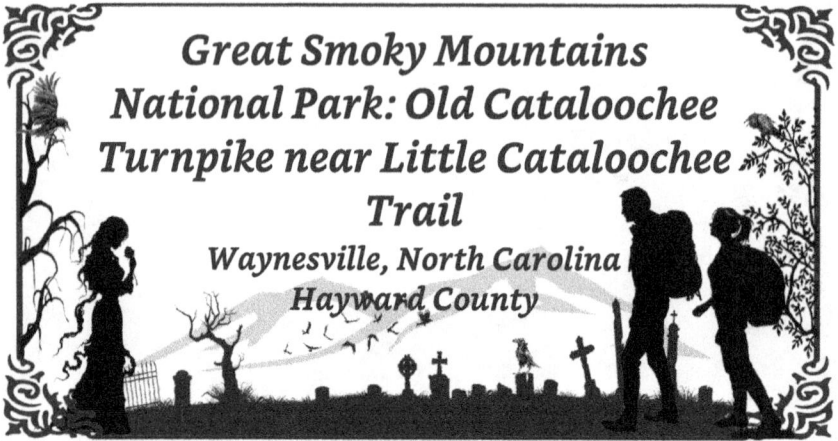

Great Smoky Mountains National Park: Old Cataloochee Turnpike near Little Cataloochee Trail

Waynesville, North Carolina
Hayward County

Last Song of the Fiddler

Along the Old Cataloochee Turnpike—

During the Civil War, small communities in Tennessee and North Carolina were divided in loyalties between the Union and the Confederacy just as they were around all states. Fighting, skirmishing, and raiding by both sides seemed unending. But, then, in April of 1864, an event stood out amongst others because of the haunting tune played before an execution—and it still lingers in the air today.

Around 1860, a rough road was etched out of the forest in the Great Smoky Mountains of North Carolina and called Cataloochee Turnpike. The narrow, twisty road was built to move livestock more easily to the eastern markets. Unfortunately, it also made it less difficult for Confederate Captain Albert Teague and his scouts to raid and harass Union sympathizers close to its path. And in late April of 1864, 28-year-old Henry Grooms, along with his brother, 30-year-old George Wiley Grooms (a private in the 11th Tennessee Cavalry of the US Army) and brother-in-law 21-year-old Mitchell Caldwell, an intellectually disabled man, were captured while working in the fields by Home Guard led by Teague.

The three men were marched along that same road in the Cataloochee Valley until they stopped by a small creek along an old Indian Trail. There, the captors told Henry (who had been clutching his fiddle as he had been forced to bring it with him) that he must play a tune.

He agreed and must have known he was standing in front of his firing squad because he played Bonaparte's Retreat, his favorite tune but slowed it down to a mournful, haunting delivery. Henry then asked his captors if he could pray before the execution. George, it seems, died cursing the Home Guards, and Mitchell's grinning at his captors so unnerved them, they made him cover his face with his hat before shooting him dead. Henry Grooms wife took an ox sled up to the place they had been murdered and brought them back to Sutton Cemetery. The fiddle was found at the dead man's feet. They were buried in a common grave with a marker stating, MURDERED. For years, those traveling the Old Cataloochee Turnpike and hikers along the Little Cataloochee Trail have heard the mournful sound of a fiddle playing. The song is Bonaparte's Retreat.

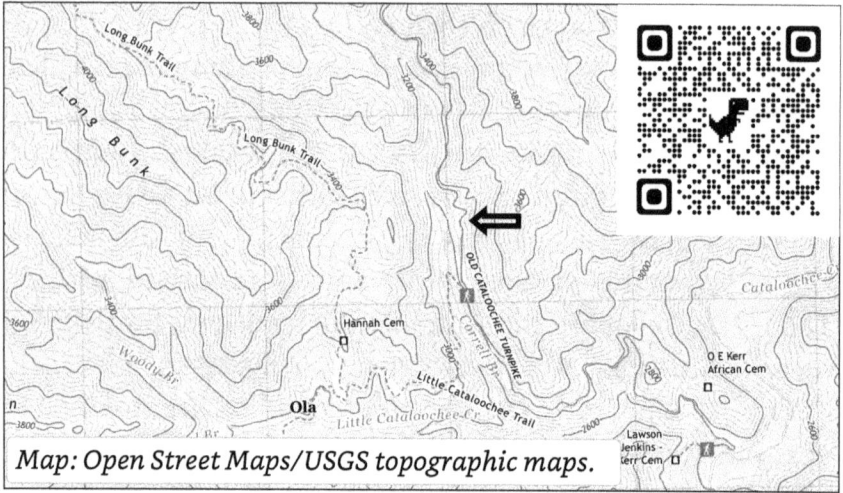

Map: Open Street Maps/USGS topographic maps.

The place of the murder is about 0.3 miles north of **Little Cataloochee Trail,** where the road crosses a small creek. This is where the Old Indian Trail and Old Indian Grave were located on early maps—(35.680084, -83.087114)

Little Cataloochee Trailhead - Waynesville, NC 28785 (35.676163, -83.087259)

A note: Mount Sterling Road (dirt) and Old Cataloochee Road (gravel) are very narrow, winding, and made for only one car and along high cliff areas. At points, you may have to pull over or back up for a long time so that others may pass and it is terrifying backing up around the narrow curves. It is a white-knuckle ride that most people will not be comfortable driving as you cannot see around many of the hairpin turns.

While you are there, Smoky Mountain National Park has trails leading to several historic cabins—one near the area of the Old Indian Trail—Little Cataloochee Trail.

Another note: The Little Cataloochee Turnpike is also closed seasonally, and you may have to hike the 4.7 miles (one-way) to the site from the location it intersects with Mt. Sterling Road. However, those who have passed along the legend say that just about anywhere on the Cataloochee Turnpike, the sound of the fiddle may be heard.

*A side note worth mentioning: There are references by some family members that George Grooms, not Henry, was the fiddle player—

Kentucky

Cumberland Falls State Resort Park— Moonbeam Trail
Williamsburg, Kentucky
Whitley County

Cumberland Falls Ghost Bride

View from Lover's Leap Overlook to watch for a ghostly bride who haunts Cumberland Falls—

During the mid-1900s, a young couple was married at Cumberland Falls outside Corbin, the groom wearing a refined dark suit, and she was donning an elegant and long white gown of silk and lace. They were madly and deeply in love and had waited a long time to be wed, scrimping and saving every penny so they could afford to be married at the falls and honeymoon at the celebrated lodge.

It was a dream come true for the two and trying to hold on to the moment as long as they could, they walked hand in hand near the waterfall. Along with him, the groom had brought a camera, and he asked his bride if she would stand near the falls so he could take her picture and remember this long-awaited moment. As the bride blushed, she did as he asked and stood along the cliff edge, posing gracefully. A gust of wind swept up the valley, and her dress whipped outward. She reached down to catch a piece of the soft material to keep it from flapping, but as she bent, the bride lost her footing. In an instant, the woman stumbled backward, tumbled from the cliff edge, and thudded sickeningly off some rocks below. Then, as the groom rushed forward, he watched her writhe with what life was left in her body. He could do nothing to save her as she wriggled off the rock ledge and into the fast-moving current of the falls, where she drowned.

There are several side-trails leading to overlooks of the falls, and perhaps the ghost!

Since then, some have beheld this ghostly bride standing where the Moonbeam Trail leads to Lover's Leap. She is seen on the cliff above the Cumberland River, a white figure in a tattered and muddy dress. She has been witnessed at the waterfall, including when the unique moonbow or lunar rainbow appears on certain full-moon and clear nights, as the mist rising off the waterfall reflects off the moon at the base of the falls and arcs downstream. Others, though, have not necessarily seen the unfortunate bride; they have heard her—while walking along the trail at dusk, a muffled scream followed by the ghastly sound of a body hitting rocks echoes up from below.

Well-marked trails are maintained, have interpretive signs on the area and its history, and they are easy to walk. Some areas are wheelchair accessible.

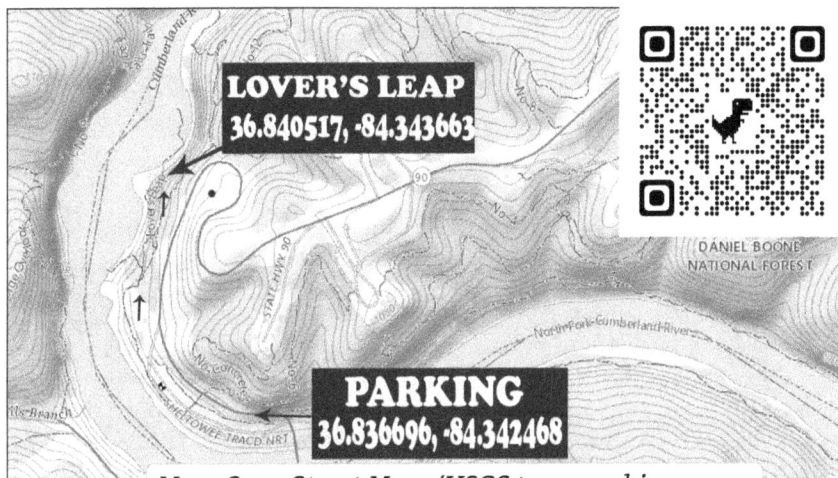

LOVER'S LEAP
36.840517, -84.343663

PARKING
36.836696, -84.342468

Map: Open Street Maps/USGS topographic maps.

Parking: Visitor Center Parking Lot
Cumberland Falls Road
Williamsburg, KY 40769
(36.836696, -84.342468)

Trail: **Moonbeam Trail to Lover's Leap Overlook**: 0.2 Miles from Visitor Center. Short series of easy steps. Easy. Out and back. Well-marked trail with informative signs. (You can continue the hike along Moonbeam Trail nearly 11 miles for a longer trek.) There is also a wheelchair accessible viewing trail.

Lover's Leap Overlook: Is located where the Dupont stone monument is located: (36.840517, -84.343663)

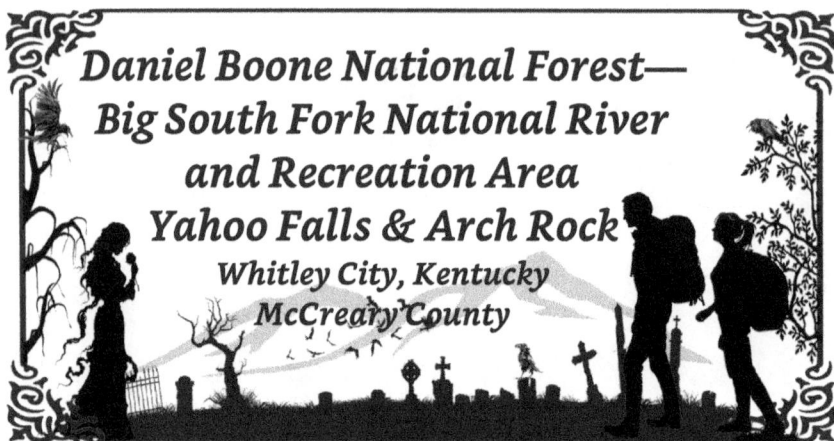

Daniel Boone National Forest—
Big South Fork National River
and Recreation Area
Yahoo Falls & Arch Rock
Whitley City, Kentucky
McCreary County

Massacre at Yahoo (Ywahoo) Falls

Yahoo Falls—

This story has been passed down by the Cherokee who once made the land we call Kentucky and Tennessee their home—

In the early 1800s, the tensions between settlers and Cherokee were at a breaking point. So the daughter of Thunderbolt War Chief Doublehead, called War Woman Cornblossom, prepared to lead the remaining children of her people in Kentucky and Northern Tennessee to a safe place that her father had arranged before he was killed.

First, he planned to organize a meeting place at a central location. Then, with the protection of Cherokee guards, the children would journey to the safety of a white-run school—a Presbyterian Indian School outside of Chattanooga directed by Reverend Gideon Blackburn.

The recess cave at Ywahoo Falls was meant to be a safe meeting area.

Soon the families had led their children to this central location, the sacred falls called Ywahoo Falls, and many had gathered there by the summer of 1810. But safe, it was not. A miscreant group of hardened Indian fighters under the guidance of Hiram Gregory got word of the peaceful gathering of the children and their mothers and decided it would be an easy murder spree, hunting the vulnerable group down and killing them in cold blood.

This was not the first time these men targeted what they deemed easy prey—Cherokee mothers, their children, and pregnant women. It was their mission. After the Revolutionary War, a state was established called Franklin in Tennessee whose inhabitants became obsessed with forcibly seizing Cherokee lands to take as their own.

Hiram Gregory had been a militiaman in the community. Among their beliefs was that if they destroyed the Cherokee young, there would be no one to run the Nation in the future. And so Gregory and his men made their way to Ywahoo Falls and tortured and murdered the over one-hundred women and children within.

Although the Cherokee account ends there, those who pass beneath the falls, now called Yahoo Falls, have mysterious encounters. Occasionally, hikers pause in their steps, hearing the low and resonating sound of singing and drumming, and even the soft cries of the children who never made it to safety.

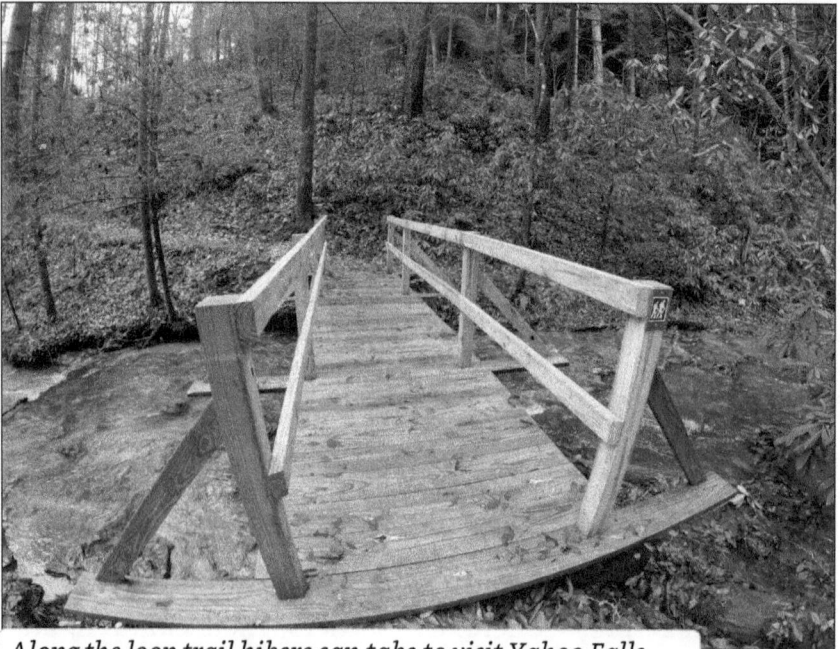

Along the loop trail hikers can take to visit Yahoo Falls.

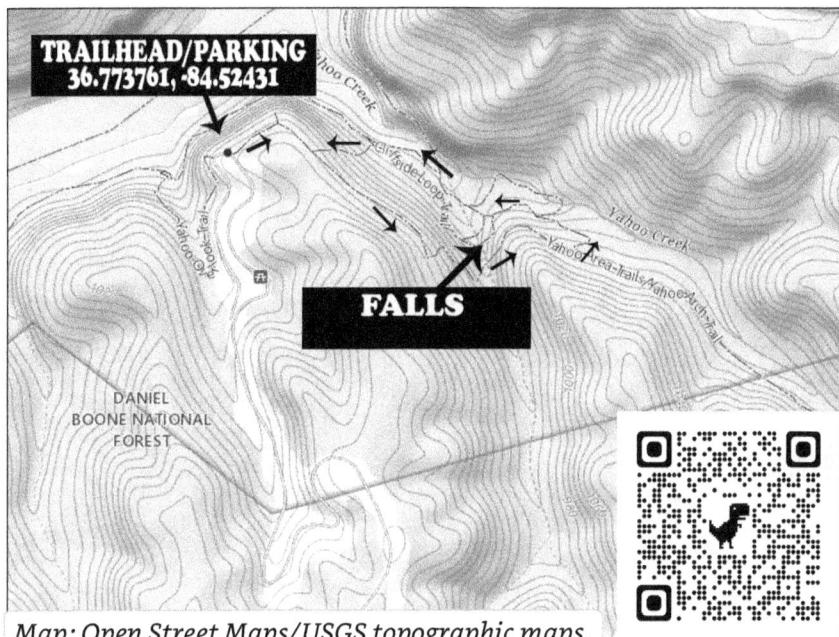

TRAILHEAD/PARKING
36.773761, -84.52431

FALLS

DANIEL
BOONE NATIONAL
FOREST

Map: Open Street Maps/USGS topographic maps.

Trailhead

Parking: Yahoo Falls Scenic Area
Yahoo Falls Road
Whitley City, KY 42653
(36.773761, -84.52431)

Trail: 1.0 miles. Loop. Hikers trek underneath the 113 foot waterfall and a large rock shelter. There are a set of steep metal steps along with a couple of creek crossings.
Yahoo Falls: (36.7726213, -84.5194249)

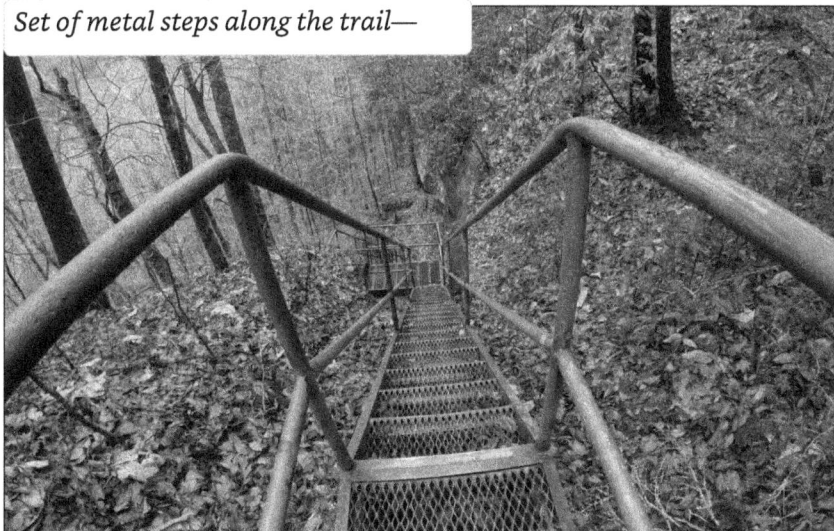

Set of metal steps along the trail—

From the loop, you can also hike 0.7 miles to Yahoo
Arch.
Yahoo Arch
Whitley City, KY 42653
(36.768101, -84.511774)

Carter Caves State Resort Park
X Cave Tour &
Horn Hollow Trail
Olive Hill, Kentucky
Carter County

Ill-starred Lovers of Carter Caves

The trail inside X Cave (two narrow passageways with entrances that meet in the center, like an X) that can be seen via a tour guide. It has a ghostly legend attached to it—

During the mid-1700s and in the region of Carter's Cave, a young Cherokee named Huraken was smitten by the chief's daughter, Manuita. He found a rich vein of silver, and he knew if he could melt the raw material, he could make many trinkets for Manuita, his love. Then one day, Huraken went off to battle. When he did not return for a long time, the people believed he had died. In her grief, Manuita jumped off a cliff.

But Huraken had not been lost in battle at all. Instead, he had snuck off to mine the silver. And when he returned, it was the same day Manuita had tossed herself from the cliff. As the young man passed the ridge on his way home, he found the dead body of his love. He carried her within a cave, now called X Cave, to watch over her.

Lover's Leap at the cave—

But when a family member found that she had gone, a search party was sent out. And they found the young woman's body with Huraken and believed he had killed Manuita. He was captured and begged to be given one last chance to see his beloved. His wish was granted. He returned to the cave but never came back out. To this day, no one knows where young Huraken vanished. The Cherokee left, believing the cave to be a bad omen.

Manuita's body was removed. But her spirit still roams the dark corners of X Cave at Carter Caves. Even hikers as far back as the 1960s walking the creek observed the pale form of an Indian woman falling from the cliff.

A section of a video I took while standing beneath Lover's Leap—a ghostly image— You can hike the Horn Hollow Trail that wanders beneath Lover's Leap.

My son and I stayed at the park and took a cave tour. After the excursion, we explored below so I could take some pictures of the area witnesses had seen the ghost. While he mucked around in the creek, I took out my camera and began to take some videos. I did not see anything strange until I got home and leafed through the videos. But then something stood out—a white figure standing stoic and alone along the cliff edge, and I could see it turning at a snail's pace. It was where no people could have hiked and was curiously pale. It was, I believe, Manuita—

Map: Open Street Maps/USGS topographic maps.

Trailheads—

Parking: Carter Caves Welcome Center (Tour for the cave starts near the parking area and tickets are picked up here.) Trailhead for Horn Hollow Trail that goes below Lover's Leap.
Ic-8024A Road
Olive Hill, KY 41164
(38.377389, -83.122906)

Trail 1: Guided tours of X Cave are offered. About 45 minutes where you walk by Lover's Leap. 0.25 miles long, 75 steps and narrow passages with stooping.

Trail 2: Horn Hollow Trail. 1.5 miles. Loop. Moderate. Hilly. Grab a permit at the Visitor Center to see a cave. The view of Lover's Leap from the trail is at the point the path crosses the creek with a bridge. Trail is marked with green blazes.

West Virginia

North Bend Rail Trail

The North Bend Rail Trail stretches 72 miles in north-central and western West Virginia. It is a wilderness pathway taking travelers across 36 bridges and through 10 tunnels. Some of those tunnels are haunted.

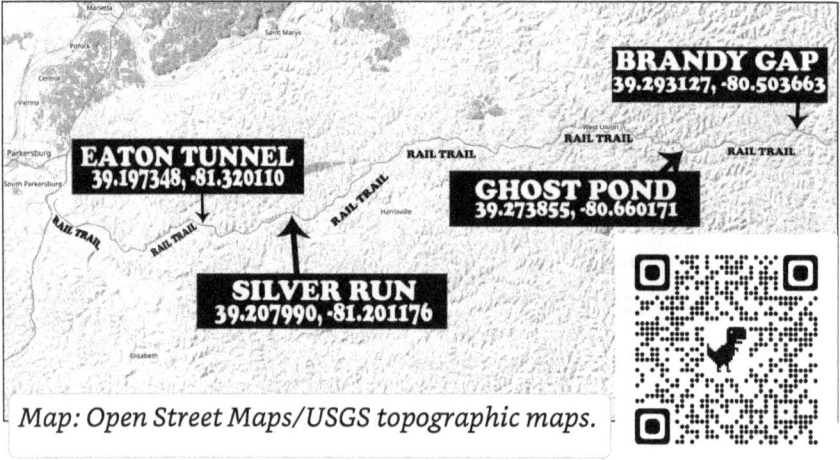

BRANDY GAP
39.293127, -80.503663

RAIL TRAIL

RAIL TRAIL

EATON TUNNEL
39.197348, -81.320110

RAIL TRAIL

GHOST POND
39.273855, -80.660171

SILVER RUN
39.207990, -81.201176

Map: Open Street Maps/USGS topographic maps.

(This map shows the long range of the North Bend Rail Trail—unless you want to hike 50 miles, you would need to drive to each haunted area.)

North Bend Rail Trail—
Section Trail to Eaton &
Lost Tunnels #21
Walker, West Virginia
Wood County

Lost Tunnel

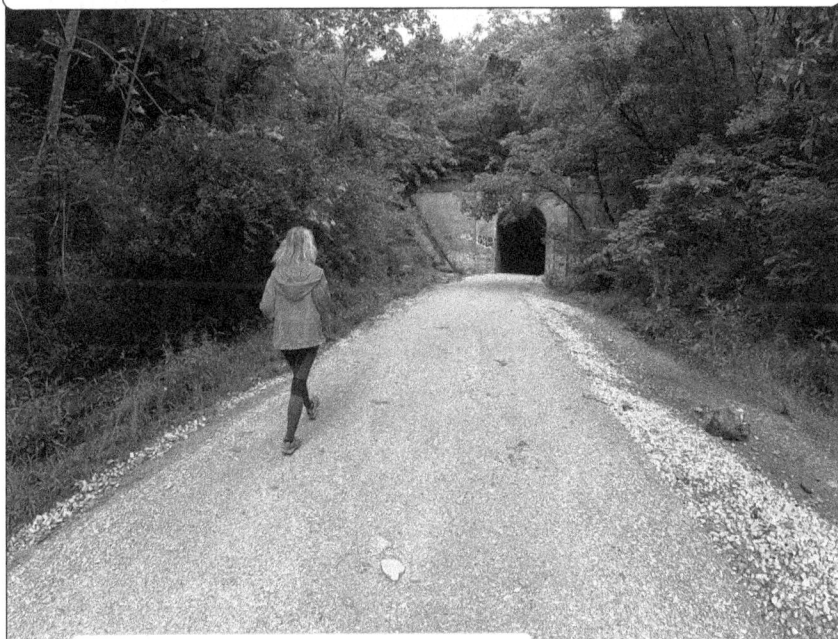

Hiking to Eaton and Lost Tunnel—

There are two tunnels secreted along the abandoned stretch of railway between Walker and Petroleum. The railway sealed one and entering is forbidden. The second, hikers can walk the graveled stretch of the old railroad bed, to explore a haunting. Both are side by side.

Standing in front of Lost/Beetree Tunnel—To get a peek at the Lost Tunnel (also #21, but the one that caved-in) you walk through the Eaton Tunnel and on the left side there is a short, rugged trail leading to the old tunnel.

The oldest and forbidden tunnel, called the Beetree Tunnel, began its existence in 1851 as part of a railway from Grafton to Parkersburg, known as the Parkersburg Branch. In 1963, two men died during a massive rockfall while widening portions of the roof. Rescuers were never able to make it to one of those workers and sealed the tunnel with the dead man inside. Beetree has come to be known as Lost Tunnel.

The railway built a second tunnel next to it. Hikers can trek this newer passageway, called Eaton Tunnel, as part of the North Bend Rail Trail. It is this newer Eaton Tunnel that some have come face to face with ghosts. As early as 1855, deaths occurred in one or the other tunnel. On January 8 of that year, Terry Duffy was in charge of the rope that sent buckets of rock to the surface. One of the cables was accidentally let loose by a worker. As the attached hook passed by Duffy, it caught his clothing and jerked him up the shaft. There, the poor man was detached and bounced down the walls of the shaft nearly 125 feet to his death.

In August of 1865, a fall of rock left three men dead, and a woman was injured seriously. In November of 1866, the Alexandria Gazette mentioned cholera swept through the mining camp at Eaton Tunnel. Of the 100 people living there, fifteen died of the disease in less than four days. In April 1877, five tramps stealing a ride in a boxcar perished when a train wrecked in the old tunnel. The dead have come back. Hikers walking through the tunnel overheard a woman's voice calling: "Help me." They scoured the area looking for a woman who needed help, but no one was around.

The air is cool and damp within the walls of the tunnel. On one of my visits to the tunnel, each time my daughter sniffed the clammy air, there was a short lull before a soft sniff replied. We had a clear view and no one else was around. Trying to make light of it (she is dauntless, but it is a bit intimidating in the darkness at some points), I laughed it off to her and said, "Hello!" sarcastically to show her there was not anybody (or anything) else inside. There was a clear "Hello!" (that was not an echo, nor a person) in return. It was an epic failure at trying to cheer her up, but she persevered with just a roll of her eyes in the lights of our cell phone flashlights.

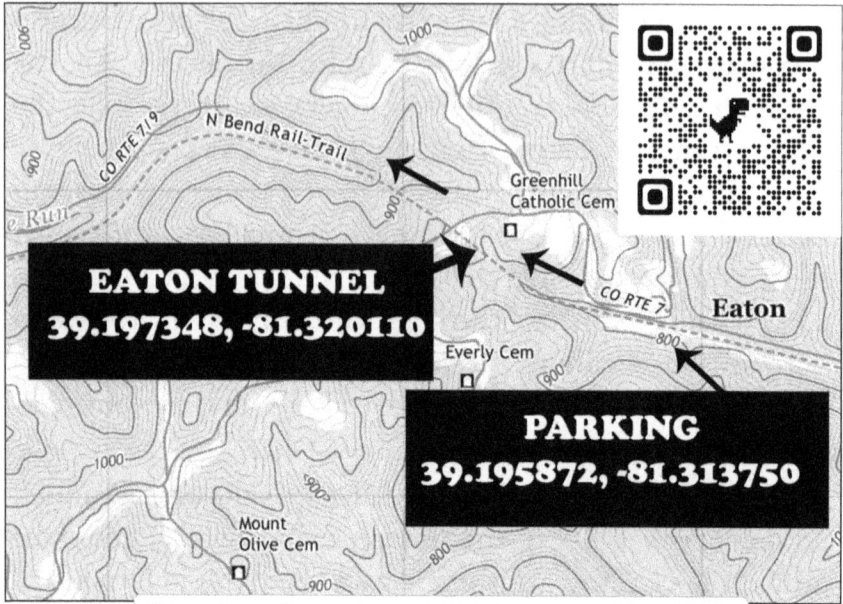

Map: Open Street Maps/USGS topographic maps.

Parking: Trail Access Parking: (39.195872, -81.313750)

Trail: Once you park, if you are facing the trail and guardrail, just hike to the right to get to Eaton Tunnel #21. Hike 0.7 miles to the far end of the tunnel (39.197348, -81.320110), where, just after look for a dirt trail leading to Lost Tunnel. Out and back. Easy.

North Bend Rail Trail— Section Trail to Silver Run Tunnel #19
Cairo, West Virginia
Ritchie County

White Woman of Silver Run

Silver Run Tunnel rail-trail—

A young woman haunts the old Baltimore and Ohio railroad just outside the town of Cairo. The tracks are torn up now, but she used to be seen walking the rails near a long, dark tunnel— An engineer was making the 169-mile midnight westbound express along the tracks starting in Grafton heading toward Clarksburg and then Parkersburg.

B & O Railroad train with cowcatcher—Image: West Virginia Regional and History Center

When the engineer came upon the short stretch of the railway at the entrance to the Silver Run Tunnel #19, in the light of the moon and headlights, he saw a woman in a pale dress with raven-colored hair and golden slippers walking along the tracks. Horrified he would hit her, he tried to stop by throwing the brakes into emergency. He could not come to a halt in time. He prayed she would step off the rail.

Suddenly, she began to glide lazily along the track away from the engine. Rattled, the engineer would later report to watchmen at the Smithburg Tunnel about 36 miles west that he and the fireman halted their run and jumped hurriedly from the train. However, a layer of fog blanketing the tracks seemed to swallow up the white woman. The conductor ran up, wondering about the emergency stop. He also helped in the search. The mysterious woman had vanished. So, they left.

The engineer had this same run every other night. He began to doubt himself thinking the ghostly woman was nothing but a wisp of fog. When his express train ran the next time, she appeared again. The engineer was ready and took in every feature of the mysterious dark-haired woman. She was dressed in a white gown with a jeweled brooch pinned to the neckline and wearing golden slippers. He threw on the brakes, and the train came to a halt. The conductor, engineer, and fireman again searched the tracks. Once more, she faded into the fog bank, but this time with a horrible, heart-wrenching moan.

As rumors about the ghostly woman made their way through the railyards, another engineer by the name of O'Flannery laughed openly at the tale and swore if he saw the woman at Tunnel #19, "I'll drive right through her!" And such on a foggy night, she was there on the tracks as if waiting for the disbeliever. O'Flannery was good to his word and did not put on the brake. He blew right through the wispy woman in white.

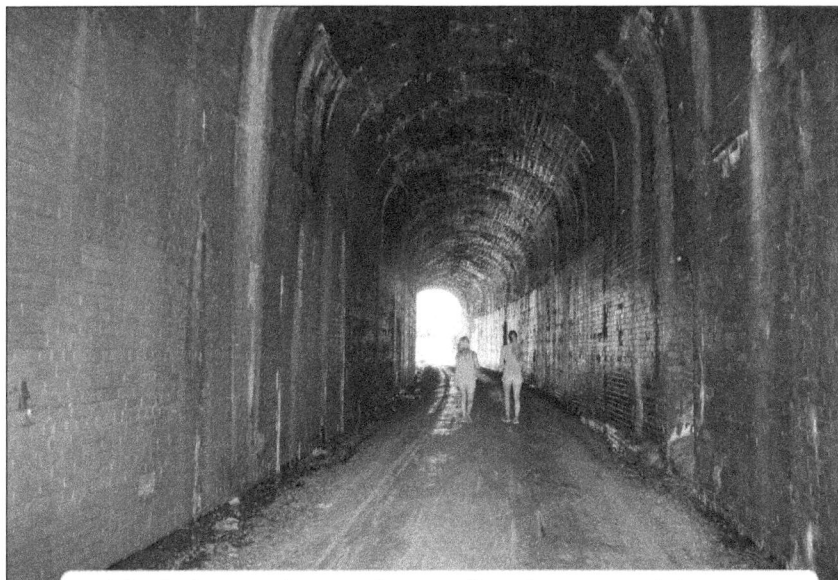

Inside the haunted Tunnel #19, Silver Run Tunnel. I suggest you bring a flashlight—it is 1376 feet long and mostly dark.

O'Flannery was quite smug until he got to Parkersburg. There he received the news that telegraphers, signalmen, and section men all along the route were reporting a pallid-faced young woman riding his cowcatcher the entire trip. She had jet-black hair and was wearing a white gown with a jeweled brooch pinned to the neckline and golden slippers!

For many years, rail men would recall seeing the ghostly woman on the tracks and hearing her moans while they drove hard through Tunnel #19. Sometime later, the young engineer who had gotten old heard that the skeleton of a woman had been found by workmen digging beside an ancient cellar at the ruins of a house near the tracks.

The rural rails along the old Baltimore and Ohio track from Parkersburg to Clarksburg no longer ring out with the shrill squeal of steel wheel to rail. The trains stopped coming, and the railway pulled the tracks in 1985. The blast of a horn through old mining and rail towns are just ghostly echoes of the past. The White Woman of Silver Run may not be riding the cowcatchers of trains anymore, but you can see her float along the path or hear a ghostly sound of a long -gone train's whistle followed by a deep moan. The Silver Run Tunnel is part of the North Bend Rail Trail system that you can hike right through the middle.

Map: Open Street Maps/USGS topographic maps.

Parking: Cairo Town Square
(39.208828, -81.156308)

Trail: Hike from downtown Cairo along the rail-trail through the tunnel about 2.8 miles (one-way). Easy. Out and back.

Begin at North Bend Rail-Trailhead at the bridge by the Bank of Cairo
4194 Main St, Cairo, WV 26337
(39.208469, -81.156517)

End at Tunnel #19, Silver Run Tunnel:
(39.207990, -81.201176)

North Bend Rail Trail—
Section Trail Along the Long Run
New Milton, West Virginia
Doddridge County

Ghost Pond on the Long Run

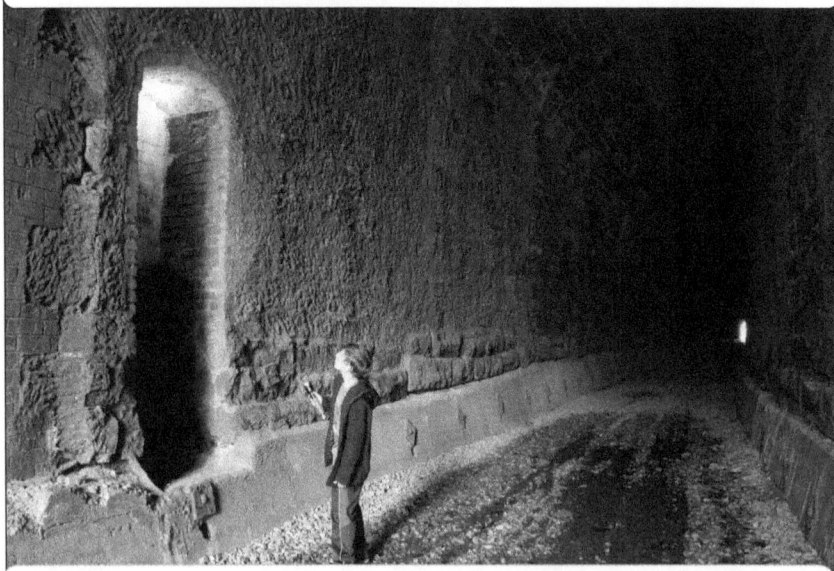

Sherwood Tunnel. There are two tunnels on this hike. One is Sherwood Tunnel and along the rail trail. You will go through this tunnel only. The other is on private property and must be viewed from the hiking trail.

In the 1920s, James Powell lived on a small farm along the Long Run in a sparsely settled community not far from Salem in Doddridge County. He was a widower and farmer, living alone in a small house and keeping mostly to himself except to go to Clarksburg occasionally to sell native medicinal herbs that he collected.

Two days before Christmas of 1924, three local boys, unemployed and desperate for Christmas money, broke into his home brandishing red bandanas to cover their identity. They held him at bay with a gun, rifled through his pockets, and robbed him of sixty-five dollars, a ring, and a watch. One small, cherished keepsake item remained in his pocket—a gold coin Powell had managed to secret. As it was about to be discovered, James Powell made a move to stop the thieves from taking the coin. One of the boys became enraged and shot the old man, killing him.

Courts later convicted the trio of murder, and police hauled the murderers away to Moundsville Prison. Powell's family laid the man to rest. His son-in-law and daughter buried his blood-stained clothing near his cabin. However, during heavy rain, the clothes were unearthed and washed into a pond nearby. Soon after, the couple reported seeing the ghostly head and neck of Powell breaking the water's surface. A great ball of fire burst from the apparition's forehead with darts shooting skyward like a Roman candle.

Rumors spread of the bizarre incident, inciting spectators to visit the site. Some would witness the ghostly form of the old man slipping up from the pond and wandering along the old train tracks that ran beside the Long Run stream. The ghost strolled through the tunnels, mumbling undistinguishable words, before vanishing from sight. A reporter from the Sandusky Star Journal picked up the story in 1927 and wrote about a man who heard voices coming from the tunnel—whispers described as too soft and garbled to comprehend. He followed the sounds to one of the indentations in the tunnel wall called a manhole— depressions inside the walls made so a person within the tunnel could escape if a train passed. He expected someone to be inside. He lit a match to peer within; no one was there.

Ghost Pond and nearby Tunnel #3 are on private property and must be viewed from the Rail Trail. To see them without going off-trail, you will need to take the hike in late fall and winter when the leaves are off the trees.

Map: Open Street Maps/USGS topographic maps.

Parking:
Long Run Road
New Milton, WV 26411
(39.280106, -80.677452)
Or (39.279672, -80.678311)

Trail: Out and back. Rail-trail. Easy. Mostly flat. 1.1 mile (one-way)
North Bend Rail-Trail
New Milton, WV 26411
Trailhead: (39.279788, -80.677318)
To (39.273855, -80.660171)

North Bend Rail Trail— Section Trail to Flinderation/ Brandy Gap Tunnel #2
Salem, West Virginia
Harrison County

Tunnel of the Dead

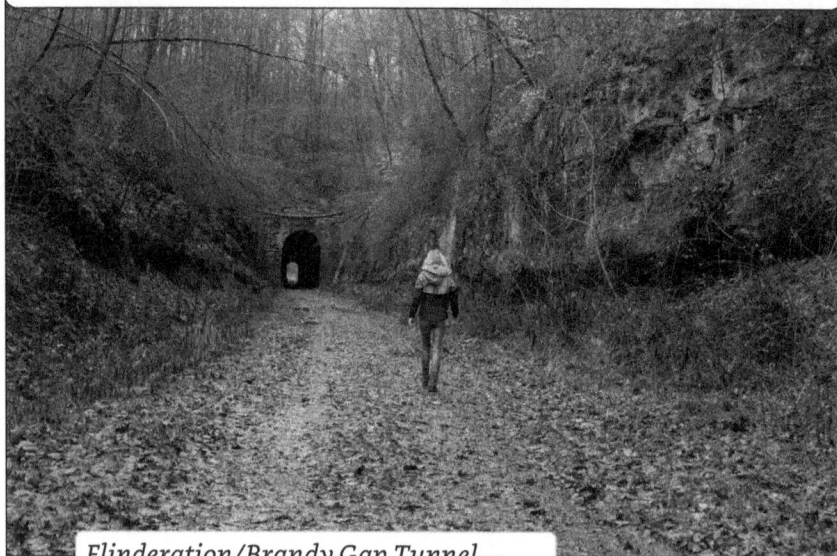

Flinderation/Brandy Gap Tunnel—

The mountains deep in West Virginia are full of old folklore, legends, and ghost stories. Many arose during the peak of the railroad, timber, and mining years when lumber and coal camps popped up along routes the trains traveled. Those living within the camps had run-ins with spirits, and their spooky stories have been passed along from one generation to the next.

If it as been raining, I recommend muck boots and an umbrella; there is an old church cemetery above the tunnel and it drips from above and puddles below. Need I say more?

There is one particular place, an especially dark one, along the West Virginia North Bend Rail Trail near Salem where such a story arose. It is called Flinderation or Brandy Gap Tunnel. The tunnel was part of the Northwestern Virginia Railroad for the Baltimore and Ohio and served as a connection between Grafton and Parkersburg. Throughout the years, there have been many accounts of strange voices, sobbing, and chatter heard within the tunnel. Even when laborers were digging through the mountain from 1852 to 1857, they reported strange lights and odd sounds inside its dark recesses.

It was not easy keeping workers in this section even when the bosses scoffed at the men for being so superstitious—there was a certain amount of discontent involved with digging so close to the cemetery belonging to Enon Baptist Church settled on the hillside above the tunnel.

Some attributed the voices to the dead in that graveyard because their everlasting rest had been disturbed by all the clamor and digging below. Still, others say they came from one of their own, a worker, whose untimely death occurred on a cold winter's day in January of 1853—

Hanley died while working on the tunnel in its very early years. Fellow workers began to hear his ghostly chatter not long after. Whether they were comforted by it or felt fear, we will not know. They, too, are dead and gone. Maybe they have returned to keep their fallen comrade company. Or perhaps they simply want to keep unwary hikers away from whatever lurks just above.

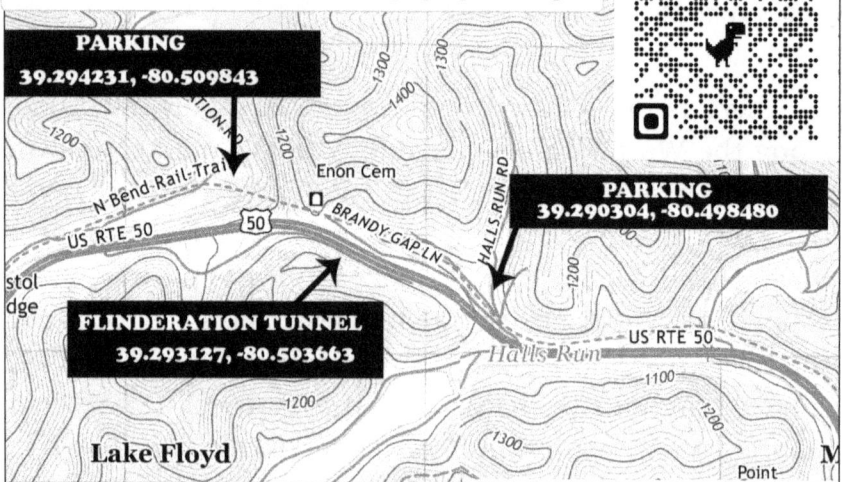

Map: Open Street Maps/USGS topographic maps.

PARKING
39.294231, -80.509843

PARKING
39.290304, -80.498480

FLINDERATION TUNNEL
39.293127, -80.503663

Parking:
There are 2 parking areas:
-**Pine Valley/Tunnel Drive**
(39.290304, -80.498480)
-**Flinderation Road**
(39.294231, -80.509843)

Trail: Flinderation/Brandy Gap Tunnel #2—0.3 miles. Out and back. Rail trail. (39.293127, -80.503663)

More Trails Around the Appalachian Region of West Virginia

Droop Mountain Battlefield State Park— The Eight Battlefield Trails

Hillsboro, West Virginia
Pocahontas County

Dead Horses and Headless Soldiers on Droop Mountain

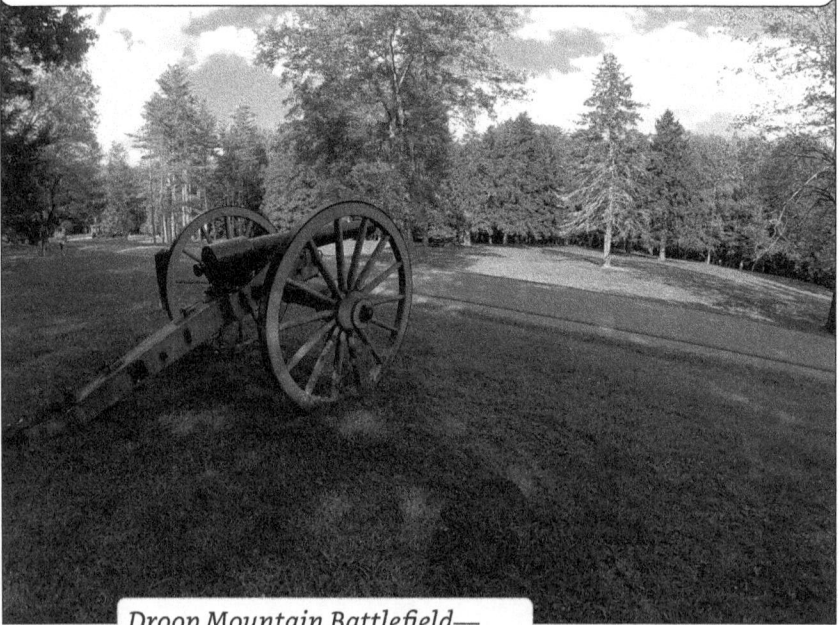

Droop Mountain Battlefield—

In November of 1863, the Union army advanced towards Salem, Virginia on a planned raid to disrupt the Virginia & Tennessee Railroad. They were waylaid by Confederate troops that had marched a grueling 27 miles on what is now US-219 to attempt to stop their assault.

Droop Mountain Battlefield—

The Confederate army was outnumbered, but held the high ground, blocking the highway so the Union could not advance. However, in the afternoon, the Confederate troops were overrun. It was considered a Confederate defeat. Still, the men stopped the Union troops from taking over the railroad. The fight lasted a day, much of it in hand to hand combat. The number of men who were killed or succumbed to wounds varies. At least 45 Union and 33 Confederate soldiers died. Since the clash, people have reported hearing sounds of a battle and seeing soldiers' spirits and a lone, misty horse. The pound of galloping horses echoes across the grounds and at least one person has seen a Confederate soldier settling in for a nap against a tree.

In the 1920s, Edgar Walton was one of two workers too tired to return home late one evening after logging at Droop Mountain. Instead, they decided to build a small fire and camp. Walton heard the leaves rustling and expected to see a deer foraging in the patches of grass beneath the trees.

The cemetery where a headless ghost of a Confederate soldier has been seen is by the park office.

Instead, he came face to face with the headless ghost of a Confederate soldier floating straight towards him. Just within reach, it turned toward a gate, disappearing. His story took place near the cemetery in what is now Droop Mountain Battlefield State Park.

Suzanne Stewart, a staff writer for The Pocahontas Times, covered a story of the restless ghosts at Droop Mountain, interviewing former employees of the park and found an interesting account. It seems Napoleon "Nap" Holbrook was a superintendent for Droop Mountain Battlefield, Holly River State Park, and Tomlinson Run until he retired in 1981. When his son Alan was young, the boy would help his dad out at the park, picking up garbage and cleaning up around the picnic areas. One day while he was out with his dad, the two drove back to the house for a few minutes, and while Nap ran inside, Alan played with a little toy truck, quietly and intently focusing on rolling it around the door and the handle.

As he was playing, he heard horses outside the vehicle, tromping on the ground, snorting, and making a fuss. He thought it strange, the sound of galloping. When he looked up, there was nothing there. Then, just as he started to tend to his little toy again, he could hear horse hooves clomping up right next to the truck. Alan looked up, horrified. He distinctly heard a horse snort loudly, felt the tepid spray of slobber hit his cheeks while the breath blew back his hair. Nothing was there. Alan's screams brought the family quickly to the truck. It would be half a week before he would come outside without crying, and for years the ghostly memory of that moment lingered in his mind.

Park Office:
683 Droop Park Road
Hillsboro, West Virginia, 24946
(38.114952, -80.269527)

Eight Hiking Trails:
Big Spring Trail: 0.75 miles. Begins at the west overlook and dead-ends at a mountain spring. Out and back. Strenuous climb back.

Cranberry Bog: 0.5 miles. Easy. Begin at the park office and end at the south picnic area. Easy.

Horse Heaven Trail: 0.25 miles. Begins at the pump house near the cannon and ends at the south picnic area. The trail follows a series of small cliffs with access to Horse Heaven Rock, where horses killed in the battle were disposed. Moderately difficult.

Musket Trail: 0.5 miles. Begins near the park office and ends at the lookout tower. Moderately difficult.

Overlook Trail: 0.5 miles. Trail begins at the pump house near the cannon and ends at the park office. Features a scenic overlook and Civil War trenches and small caves. Moderately difficult.

Minie Ball Trail: 0.5 miles. Covers area where Union soldiers overtook the mountain to attack the Confederates above. Trail begins at the first sharp curve in the road near the park office and ends at the tower. Difficult.

Old Soldier Trail: 0.75 miles. Hikers take an old roadbed which passes near the spot where Major Bailey was shot rallying his men around the Confederate flag. Trail starts near the battlefield monuments and ends at the stone shed by the tower. Easy.

Tower Trail: 0.5 miles. This trail begins at the park office and ends at the stone shed by the lookout tower.

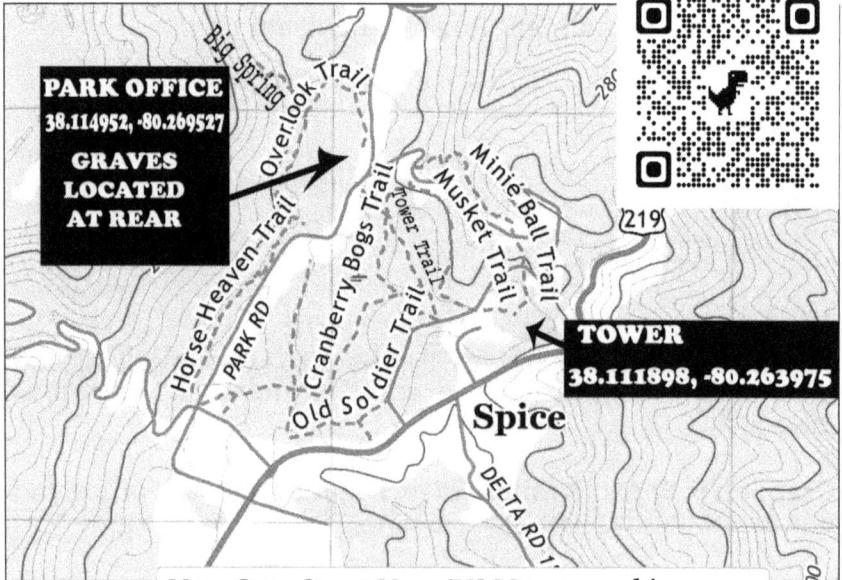

Map: Open Street Maps/USGS topographic maps.

Hatfield Family Cemetery— Cemetery Walkway
Sarah Ann, West Virginia
Logan County

Hatfield Family Rising

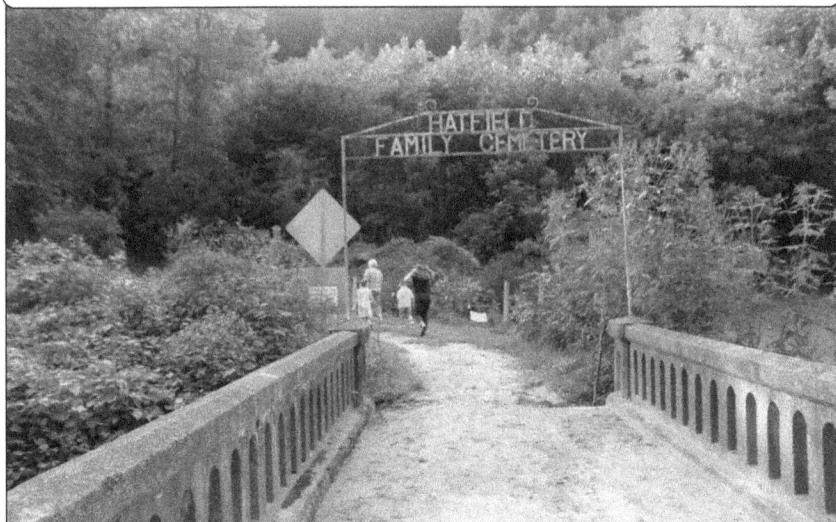

The Hatfield and McCoy families from Mingo and Logan counties in West Virginia and Pike County in Kentucky would be just two families living opposite each other on the Tug Fork of the Big Sandy River if it were not for the feud. The Randolph McCoy family lived mostly on the Pike County, Kentucky side. The family owned a 300-acre farm and livestock and dealt in illegal moonshine. Almost all the McCoys residing in the area fought for the Confederacy in the Civil War, except Asa Harmon McCoy, who was a younger brother of Randolph and who fought for the Union.

On the other side—the William Anderson "Devil Anse" Hatfield family was mainly from Mingo County, West Virginia. The Hatfields had a successful timbering business, employed more than a dozen men, sold illegal moonshine, and fought for the Confederates. They were both prominent families in a rural area and hardly much different than any other families struggling in the late 1800s during a civil war and standing on the cusp of a coal mining revolution.

That is, until 37-year-old Asa Harmon McCoy mustered out of Company E, 45th Regiment of the Kentucky Infantry for the Union side with a broken leg on December 24th of 1864. He was sent home on leave to mend his wounds. He came home to a chilly welcome from his southern sympathizing family, but it was Devil Anse Hatfield's Logan Wildcats, Confederate Home Guards, who found out he was there, dragged him out of hiding, and murdered him. After that and a few minor incidents like a disagreement over a hog, whatever relationship the families had turned rancid, and the legendary war began. They spent many years leaving a trail of beatings and burnings, stabbings and shootings across those three counties.

A legend surrounds the Hatfield Cemetery and Anse's grave below.

Anse Hatfield spent his last years quietly on his farm. Then, in 1911, he was baptized by an old friend, "Uncle Dyke" Garrett, the famous preacher who spent his life riding his old mule up and down the mountains to visit the sick and preach to those who would listen. On January 6th, 1921, at age 82, Hatfield died from pneumonia and was buried in the Hatfield Cemetery outside the town of Sarah Ann. However, the ghosts of Anse Hatfield and his sons remain. They return on foggy nights— rising from the graves. They make a quiet march down the mountain and toward the small Island Creek at the bottom. When they reach the stream, Preacher Garrett rises and baptizes them, washing away all their sins. Then, they disappear.

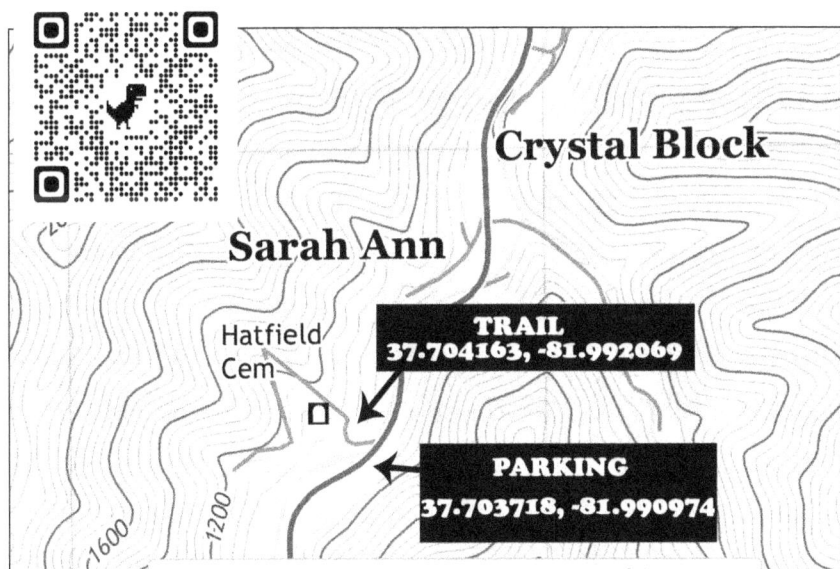

Map: Open Street Maps/USGS topographic maps.

Parking: (37.703718, -81.990974)

Trail: Hatfield Family Cemetery Access Road- 0.1 miles along cemetery access road. Easy. Out and back.
Omar, WV 25638
(37.704163, -81.992069)

Monongahela National Forest— Seneca Rocks Trail
Seneca Rocks, West Virginia
Pendleton County

Legend of Seneca Rocks

Along the base of Seneca Rocks as seen by the trailhead. You can visit and climb up the trail to an overlook.

Seneca Rocks is a cliff rising nearly 900 feet above the union of Seneca Creek and the North Fork of the South Branch of the Potomac River. It is hiked by many, climbed by some, and is shrouded in legends stemming from its grand, craggy exterior. The most famous legend, by far, is the tale of the strong Indian girl who chose her husband using the steep climb as a test of his strength—

Snowbird was the daughter of the local Indian chief, Bald Eagle and his wife, White Rock. She grew up in the shadow of Seneca Rocks and climbed to the summit quite often and always alone, for no one else at this time had conquered the high cliff. She was strong and lithe, beautiful, and intelligent. And she had a charm and wit about her that made her quite popular among the young women and men of not only her people but also neighboring tribes.

Seneca Rocks Trail —

The time had come for Snowbird to marry. Her suitors were many, and they settled into a special place beneath the Seneca Rocks where Bald Eagle bid them meet. But it was Snowbird who would raise her hand to quiet the crowd. And some were surprised it was she and not the chief who addressed them— "I am my father's only daughter. Since I was a child, my parents taught me to be strong. Often, I climb to the summit of the rocks above us to prove to myself that I am both powerful and strong. Such, I need a husband who has the same strength to offer." She took in each of her nervous suitors. They peered back at her with hopeful eyes.

"Of all of our people, I am the only one who has climbed these stones. Today, I will climb them again. Whoever is willing to risk his life for me and conquer the rocks will have a chance at my hand. To whoever wins this challenge, I will give my heart and my life." She breathed in the sweet air and thrust her chin high. "I need someone strong enough to be my husband, brave enough to follow me into adventures to the end, and generous enough to know strength comes from within and not from what is seen by the eye. Who among you will try?"

Seneca Rocks Trail is a well maintained hiking trail to an observation platform and may be crowded seasonally.

Many eyes followed Snowbird's hand, pointing to Seneca Rocks. Many of those who were weaker lowered their chins and stepped back, choosing not to follow her, not to take the challenge. Then Bald Eagle stepped up beside his daughter. He looked around. There were seven hopeful men left. "Snowbird will climb to the top of the crag today," he told them. "If one of you follows her to the peak, you will receive her hand in marriage and, perhaps, become chief one day. Let the contest begin."

A view from above as Snowbird would have seen, barring the modern homes and businesses. The name comes from the Seneca Indians, who used this area for hunting, fishing, and trade routes.

The competition began. Snowbird started the ascent up the rocks, the seven men following in her footsteps. The climb was steep, and the men breathed hard, lungs aching and sweat pouring down their brows. Two men became exhausted only a quarter of the way, pausing with hands on knees. They looked at one another and shook their heads. They could go no farther. Then they turned their backs and walked back down the way they had come. Halfway, another man dropped to the ground. He, too, shook his head and prepared to descend the mountainous terrain.

Not long after, the fourth slipped on a rock and fell, dangling by one hand almost to die. The fifth snatched his arm, saving him. The two turned on the path and left the last to follow Snowbird. The weakest of the remaining two was climbing a steep wall and slipped, falling to his death.

There was but one remaining, and he quietly clambered behind Snowbird along steep ledges, up sheer walls hand-over-hand, and across vast expanses, nearly falling to his death many times.

Finally, near dusk, Snowbird and the lone suitor were near the top, and suddenly, overcome with fatigue, the last suitor for the Indian girl slid along some stones only a stone's throw from the very top. He fell off a sharp embankment and stopped just short of the 900-foot drop, dangling precariously by one hand.

"So alone, I will be," Snowbird said softly to herself as she looked up to the peak and saw how close they were, then downward, observing the man's fingers slipping, slipping, slipping. But as she peered at him, she saw the determination in his eyes, watched as he worked his fingers trying for a better grasp. He did not give up, nor did he fear. Instead, his jaws were churning in determination, his eyes working upward to take her in as if to ask her if she was strong enough to be his wife, brave enough to share this adventure to the end, generous enough to know strength comes from within and not from what is seen by the eye.

Loneliness enveloped Snowbird. She remembered the many times she came here alone and how she had enjoyed walking with this man from the bottom of the rock to the top. She shifted, rushing downward, and took his wrist, and helped him rise from sure death. The two would finish the climb together just as they would marry and live a long and happy life and forever pass down the story of their courage.

Map: Open Street Maps/USGS topographic maps.

**Parking and
Seneca Rocks Trailhead**—(38.835598, -79.372624)

Trail: 1.5 miles (one-way). The hiking trail rises to nearly 700 feet in elevation gain and ends in an observation platform near the top of Seneca Rocks. Steep, the trail is not difficult, but has gentle uphill grades, steps, and switchbacks.

New River Gorge National Park and Preserve

The New River is one of the oldest rivers in the Americas. New River Gorge National Park and Preserve maintains 70,000 acres along its path between Hinton and Fayetteville. The park service has preserved many historical mining towns within this natural community and created hiking trails to visit them. Some have ghostly tales to tell.

New River Gorge National Park and Preserve— Southside Trail

Fayetteville, West Virginia
Fayette County

Beckoned to a Cemetery Secreted Along New River

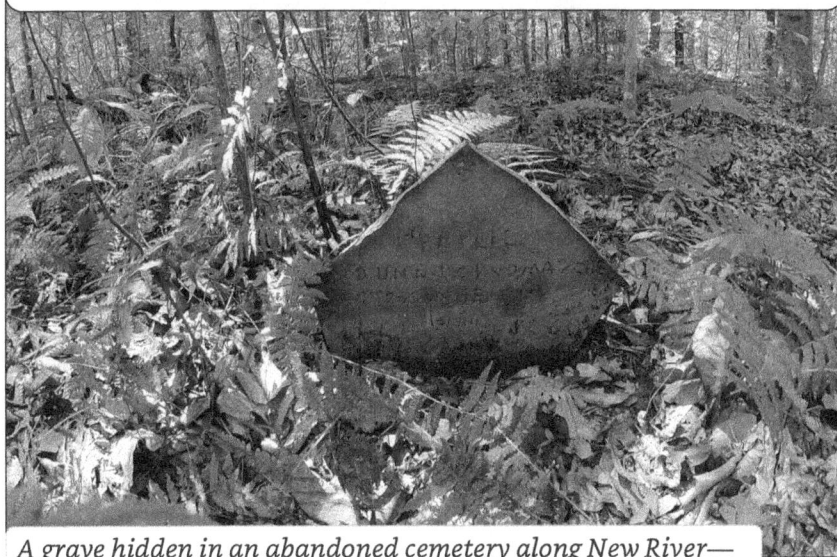

A grave hidden in an abandoned cemetery along New River—

I was out hiking the Southside Trail along the New River past some old ghost towns and heading for the long-gone community of Red Ash and its historic coke ovens. I heard what sounded like a newborn baby crying and thought it might be an uncommon bird to West Virginia on its migratory path. Occasionally I get the chance to record an odd noise that might fool people into thinking it is a ghost.

I have managed to collect quite a few like a tiny screech owl's territorial wraithlike shriek, an elk's bugling scream far-off, and the eerie grunts and clacks of wild turkey roosting in dark treetops for the night. I use them to show, in presentations, that not all things that go bump in the night are ominous. I thought I would get closer and get a clip of the sound on my phone. I set off blindly through the woods, following it for about an hour, but the bird was nowhere to be found. Then I see the orange flagging tape that hikers place on trees to mark a trail, and I look around, and lo and behold, they lead to an old cemetery.

Nearly concealed by the brush and leaves, large round stones and indentations in the earth are signs of graves.

I later found out that the land I came upon was a 12-acre island—the day I went, I just had to cross two muddy creeks. But seasonally, it is surrounded by water. Long ago, the island would have been between the railway (which is now the Southside Trail I was hiking) and New River.

It belonged to the Red Ash community, one of the first coal mining and coke manufacturing towns along the south bank of the New River in the early 1890s. During that time, there was a smallpox epidemic. Because there were no hospitals nearby that could take those who were contagious, the community built a couple of pest houses to shelter those who were ill, isolating them from others who would catch the dreaded sickness. A separate doctor's home was also erected on the island. Those who died there were buried on the island. Their graves were marked with river stones or wooden crosses.

Coke ovens and old home ruins are found along the trail—

Over the years and even past the 1920s, when the Red Ash mine closed, community members buried their dead here, including men who died in mining accidents at Red Ash, Rush Run, and Echo Mine at Beury. In March of 1900, there was an explosion in the mine at Red Ash ignited by the open flame in miners' headlamps coming into contact with methane gas. Forty-six miners were suffocated or died in the explosion and were buried here.

Red Ash 1890s—Image: NPS

Then in 1905, sparks from a mine car ignited coal dust, exploding. Thirteen miners died. Eleven men who went in to rescue them also died in a second explosion. In 1918, when the Spanish Influenza epidemic ran rampant across the U.S., young and old in these small New River mining communities may have been isolated, but not enough so that they could not escape its wrath. Again, those who died here were buried at Red Ash.

So back to that noise leading me to the burial ground and that baby's desperate shriek-cry. As soon as I got to the cemetery, it had faded away to the grind of rail to the wheel of a train across the roaring river, tree canopy waving in the wind, and the crunch of leaves beneath my feet. But just as there could have been a few strange birds flying over New River that day, there were plenty of babies buried on the island. Although I could not get a good clip of that mysterious cry over the noise of nature and railway, I would like to think that maybe my visit soothed whatever little souls were there searching for company.

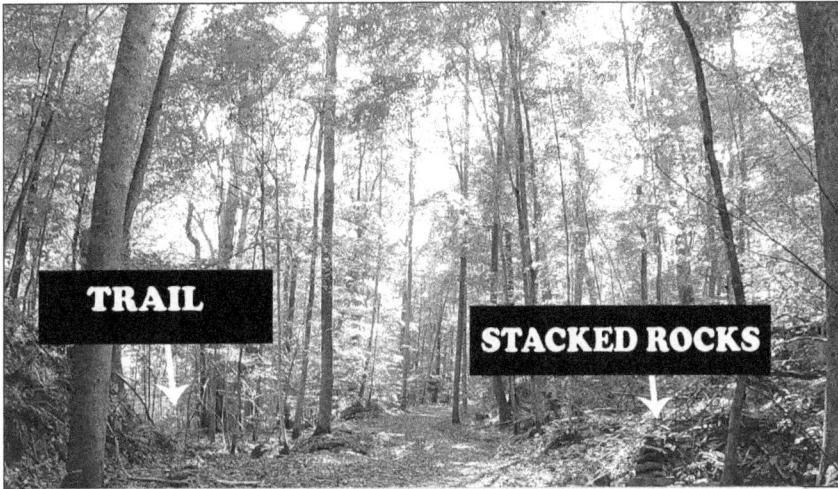

Stacked rocks (cairns) as above are properly used as trail markers indicating the path to the cemetery. It is just another motivation (including they are an eyesore, damage wildlife and kill animal species that live beneath them), to NOT stack rocks for fun and lead hikers astray. As an outdoor adventurer who gets lost in a bucket, I beg you to leave the stone stacking to those marking the trails.

Parking: **Brooklyn Campground** (Brooklyn to Southside Junction Trailhead) (37.984139, -81.028056)

Trail: Hike **Southside Trail** for about 1.4 miles. Along the way, hikers will see several ruins of homes and businesses. Watch for a knee-high stack of rocks on the right side marking the cemetery trail. The island may be surrounded by water seasonally. Aim for the sound of fast-moving water as the cemetery is near the loud rapids boaters call 'Surprise Rapid' on the river.
Cemetery: (37.964093, -81.023718)

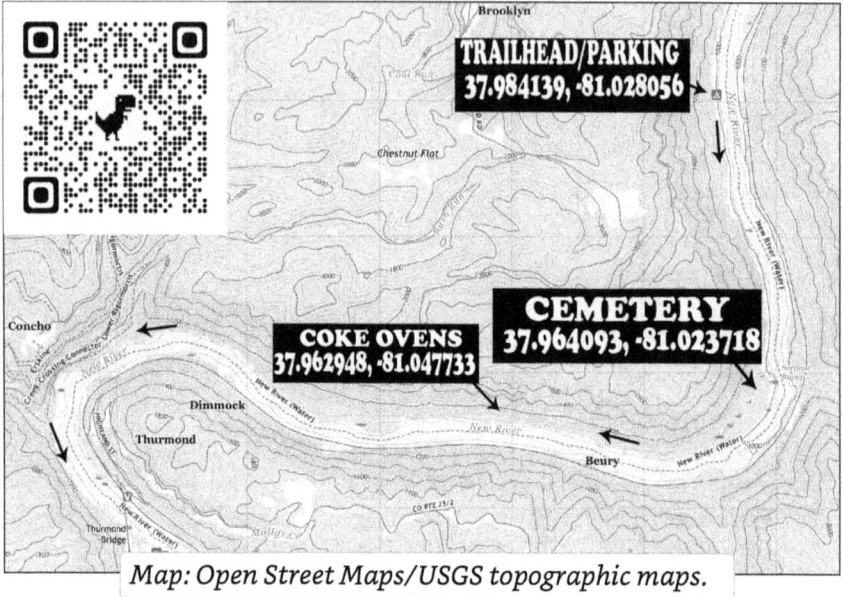

Map: Open Street Maps/USGS topographic maps.

Trail: You can continue on the Southside Trail as it weaves along the river past abandoned mining towns such as **Red Ash** and **Rush Run** to the ghost towns of **Dun Glen** and **Thurmond**, passing the Red Ash Coke Ovens (37.962948, -81.047733) at about mile 2.8.

It is a total trail route of 6.2 miles (one-way) for the trip to Thurmond. Crossing the bridge after the trail end (Dun Glen) will take you into Thurmond from Thurmond Road. Watch for train traffic. Out and back. Mostly flat.

New River Gorge National Park and Preserve— Kaymoor Miners Trail
Fayetteville, West Virginia
Fayette County

Ghost Trains and Dead Miners

Kaymoor during its heyday—Image: NPS

It is the perfect setting for a ghost story. Deep in the mountains of Fayette County, tucked along the New River and isolated from the rest of the world, is the abandoned coal and coke town of Kaymoor. A few buildings remain, crumbling and looming beneath a canopy of huge trees that cover them in eerie darkness.

The mountain is steep, overgrown, and rugged where a big town once stood. The air is fresh and scented by nature—trees, leaves, and river. However, a keen eye can pick out things from the past—old chamber pots, medicine bottles, iron furnace doors, and more partially hidden beneath the dirt. And there is silence barring the occasional train still zooming along the tracks below. This is Kaymoor now.

Kaymoor in the 1950s—NPS

Back in the day, though . . .the terrain was a bit different, and the air was filled with the chatter of people, children's laughter, the clatter, and roar of machinery, bawls of mules, and grind of train wheels on tracks. The sharp waft of coke ovens might burn the nostrils a bit, along with the hint of chimney smoke mingling with the scents of home-cooked meals. Back then, drawn in by the rich coal found in the region, the Low Moor Iron Company opened two mines around these resources in 1899. There were two sections of town, Kaymoor Top and Kaymoor Bottom. The company built fifty houses in 1901 in the community; many more were added over the next few years.

Kaymoor today—

The company employed 800 -1500 workers during peak production. Their families lived in the community along the mountainside. The company paid miners in scrip that they could only use in the company store and cash. The town encompassed little more than those homes, a pair of segregated schools, company stores, ballfield, and a pool hall. It was in operation until 1962. But by the early 1950s, most of the bottom of the town was already abandoned. Then it burned in 1962. Mines were a dangerous place to work. Roof falls, fires, and electrocutions were the primary causes of death at Kaymoor mine. By 1940, 21 men had died there. Family members probably died there too. It was far from the bigger towns with doctors and hospitals. If miners or their families were sick and in sudden need of a hospital, it was not a quick jaunt up the road.

There are stories of a ghostly steam engine running along the tracks. Those who are hiking nearby only believe it is a typical train passing until it occurs to them it stopped abruptly and disappeared. Others have seen miners walking along long-gone sidetracks who then fade away into tiny, flickering lights that suddenly wiggle and whip away before disappearing entirely.

Kaymoor today—before the steps—

On the fall day when all the other trails were packed with hikers, I was completely alone down there— or not. As I walked up the steps, I occasionally stopped to catch my breath. I swore I heard footsteps just behind like someone was trying to catch up. *Tap-tap-tap-tap.* Not just once but at every stop along the climb—until I reached the top tier. Then, only the wind played with the leaves in the trees. As I looked down into the dark bottoms below, I thought, yep, it is the perfect setting for a ghost story.

Some of the 821 (one-way) steps to get to the bottom.

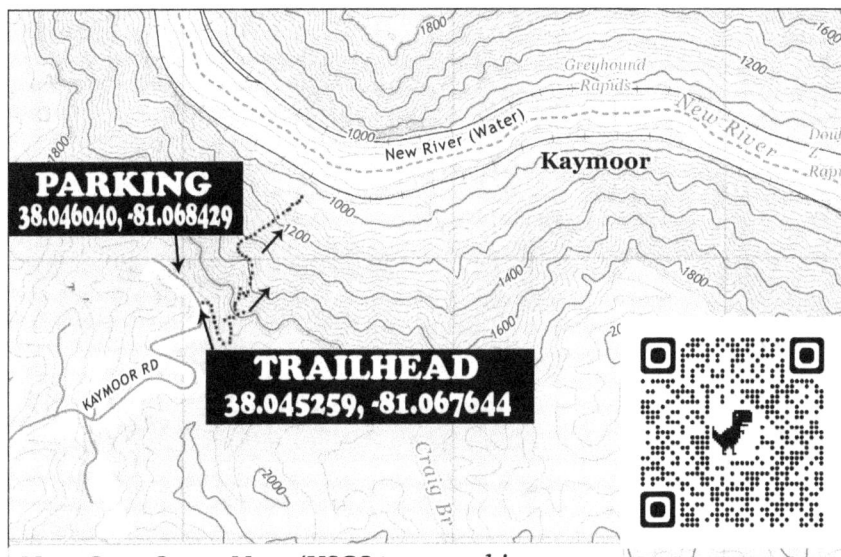

Map: Open Street Maps/USGS topographic maps.

Parking: (38.046040, -81.068429)

Trail: 1.0 miles. Out and back. Difficult. The trail is strenuous, steep, and that is only the first section. If you want to go to the very bottom, there are 821 calf-wrenching steps partway that you must take to get down to the ruins. There are 821 thigh-wrenching steps to climb back up. However, I can bet there will not be many others down there—but perhaps a few ghosts.

Kaymoor Miners Trailhead
Kaymoor Road
Fayetteville, WV 25840
(38.045259, -81.067644)

Harpers Ferry & Harpers Ferry National Historical Park— Trail to Jefferson Rock

Harpers Ferry, West Virginia
Jefferson County

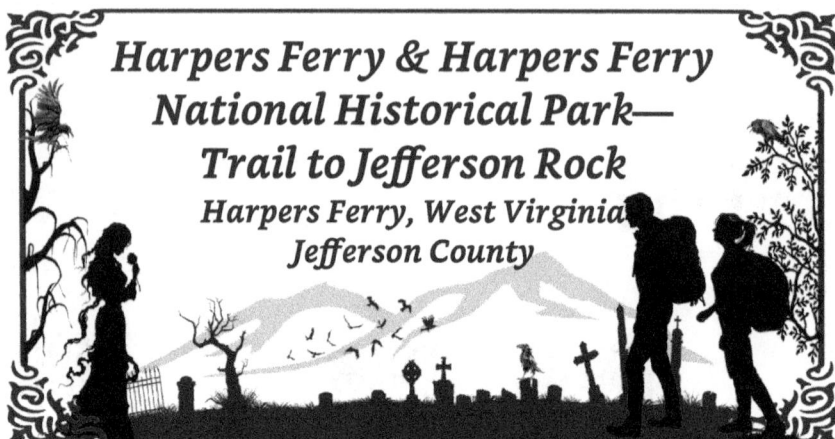

Ghosts of Harpers Ferry

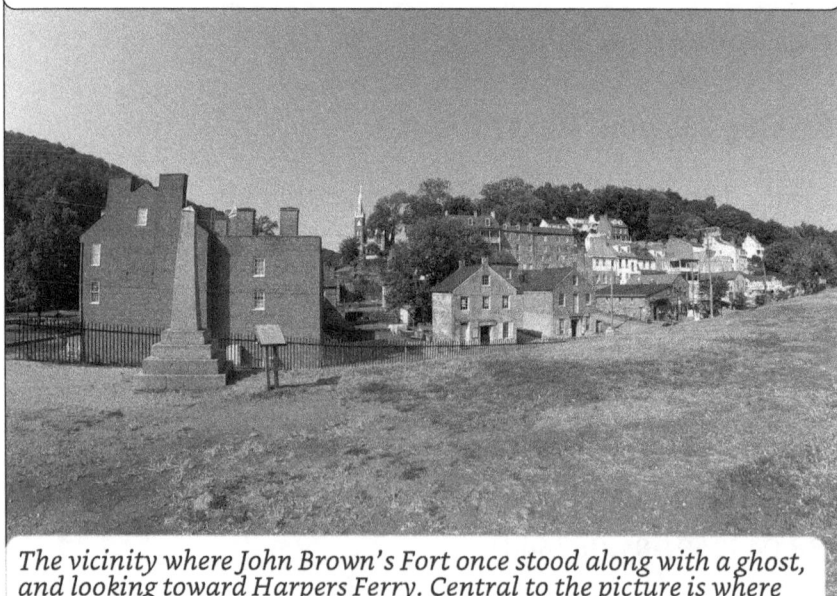

The vicinity where John Brown's Fort once stood along with a ghost, and looking toward Harpers Ferry. Central to the picture is where the stone steps lead to more spooky places.

On the night of October 16, 1859, 59-year-old John Brown led 21 men, including two of his sons, on a raid to seize the U.S. Arsenal at Harpers Ferry, where the Shenandoah and the Potomac Rivers meet. His goal was to use the guns to create a vast army of former slaves, incite a rebellion to free all enslaved people, and after that, create a separate state in the Shenandoah Valley for blacks.

He failed miserably. Even though he was hanged in Charles Town, tourists have seen his ghostly figure around the town of Harpers Ferry, usually where the fort once stood. He appears unhurried, strolling the area and appearing like one of the park's historical reenactors.

The Stone Steps—if you listen carefully, you may hear a baby cry at this location by the building, a ghostly reminder of a child killed during the Civil War—

He is not the only ghost to boldly show itself in this historical town. Hikers can take the old stone steps off High Street and along the Appalachian Trail. Before they pass St. Peter's Roman Catholic Church, if they stop for a moment quietly, they may see Father Michael Costello, the priest at St. Peter's, from 1857 to 1867, walk right out of the church's wall where a door once stood. Not a long walk from the church, hikers will pass Jefferson Rock, so named for Thomas Jefferson, who paused to enjoy the view there and place his flowery description in print. But it is not Jefferson whose ghostly presence has made a mark here.

A few years ago, a young couple stopped there well into the evening to enjoy the view and, of course, utilize the area as a lovers' lane. As they sat there, the two caught the scent of campfires burning and, most likely, reckoned it was nothing more than someone grilling late at night. But it was the sound of boots scuffing against the stone and sand path that caught their attention when they noted several figures were coming down the stone step trail. They narrowed their gaze and took in the oozy forms of three men.

The area is tree-covered and dim, even during the light of day. At night, the figures seemed to come out of nowhere, which was not considerably menacing as it was a path from Bolivar Heights and into Lower Town. However, the men wore the uniforms of Civil War soldiers, and they leaned into each other while traveling the trail. Again, the couple did not hesitate to assume the forms were historical reenactors from the town working their way home. There was a strange hint to the air, so the couple pushed to their feet and followed them along the dark footpath. Then, suddenly, and right as they came up to them, the men vanished!

Those who continue can take the connector trail back toward town, ending at The Point where the land juts out, and the Potomac and Shenandoah rivers meet. Not only can you look upon three states here—Maryland, Virginia, and West Virginia, but your walk may be interrupted by a ghostly Good Samaritan. Moses Fine was a peddler from Bolivar and Harpers Ferry in the 1920s. He was killed by a speeding drunk driver in 1923. Not long after, his ghost began showing up to warn others before horrifying accidents happened to them—and The Point seems to be his favored spot as he tends to try to stop people from going close to the raging waters and drowning.

Map: Open Street Maps/USGS topographic maps.

Parking: If available, it is usually easiest to park at the train station early morning and pay there. However, the National Park Service recommends parking at the Visitor Center Parking Lot in peak seasons: (39.316667, -77.756389) where a shuttle is available (no pets allowed).

Trail: John Brown's Fort (Original Site)
Plaque Showing Original Site of John Brown's Fort
100-116 Potomac St, Harpers Ferry, WV 25425
(39.323501, -77.729925)
Walk down Shenandoah Street and toward **the John Brown Fort**: (39.323128, -77.729611), then a block to High Street and take the steps upward:

Appalachian Trail Stone Steps:
(39.323058, -77.730706)
Pass the **St Peter's Church** and then **Jefferson Rock**, continue onward and follow the signs for the Connector Trail and back along the beautiful Shenandoah to downtown and **The Point**.

Maryland

Harpers Ferry National Historical Park— Maryland Heights Trail
Knoxville, Maryland
Washington County

Phantoms of the Mountain

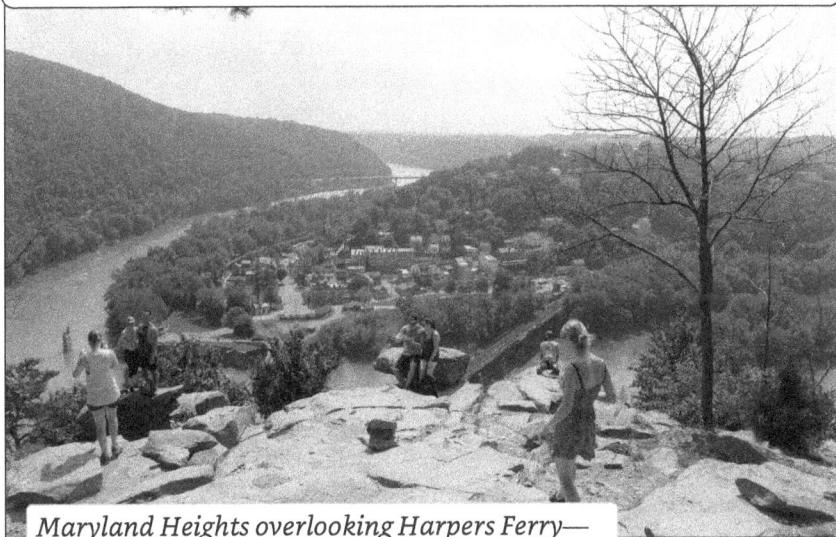

Maryland Heights overlooking Harpers Ferry—

In May of 1862, Union Troops built a defense at Maryland Heights, along Elk Ridge of the Blue Ridge Mountains, and overlooking the town of Harpers Ferry. It would become the grounds for the first battle between Union and Confederate troops in Maryland in September of 1862. The battle on the mountain lasted nine hours and ended with the Confederacy forcing the Union troops to abandon their position on Maryland Heights and descend into Harpers Ferry.

As part of the Harpers Ferry Battle, the Confederate Army had 39 killed. The Union had 44 killed, many dying on the mountain. Since, some hiking along the Maryland Heights trail have witnessed ghostly soldiers appear on the path. Believing them to be either reenactors or ardent Civil War buffs, they are stunned when the figures completely vanish. Those watching from The Point below in Harpers Ferry have seen twinkling lights along the mountainside, long-gone campfires of ghostly troops still waiting battle.

Parking: The National Park Service recommends parking at the Visitor Center Parking Lot in peak seasons: (39.316667, -77.756389) where a shuttle is available (no pets allowed).

Trail: To Overlook Cliff

From Harpers Ferry (Lower Town), you can cross the Footbridge to C&O Canal and Maryland Heights by The Point: (39.323578, -77.728822)
You will follow the canal towpath to the left until you get to a small wooden footbridge over the canal bed about 0.3 miles (39.328943, -77.731246), and directly across, you will see the trailhead for the Maryland Heights trail.
Lower Town to Maryland Heights Overlook: 4.5 miles round trip. Strenuous. Difficult. Out and back.
Maryland Heights Loop: 6.6 mile. Strenuous. Difficult. Loop.

Park map: NPS

Maryland Heights Trails
Harpers Ferry National Historical Park

National Park Service
Department of the Interior

Legend

--- Maryland Heights trails

• Interpretive sign

Appalachian Trail (white blaze)

NPS land

Information Center to trail head (one way): 0.7 mi.
Trail head to Overlook Cliff (green + red blaze) (one way): 1.4 mi.
Stone Fort Trail (blue blaze): 2.2 mi.
Hike difficulty: Difficult

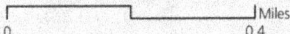

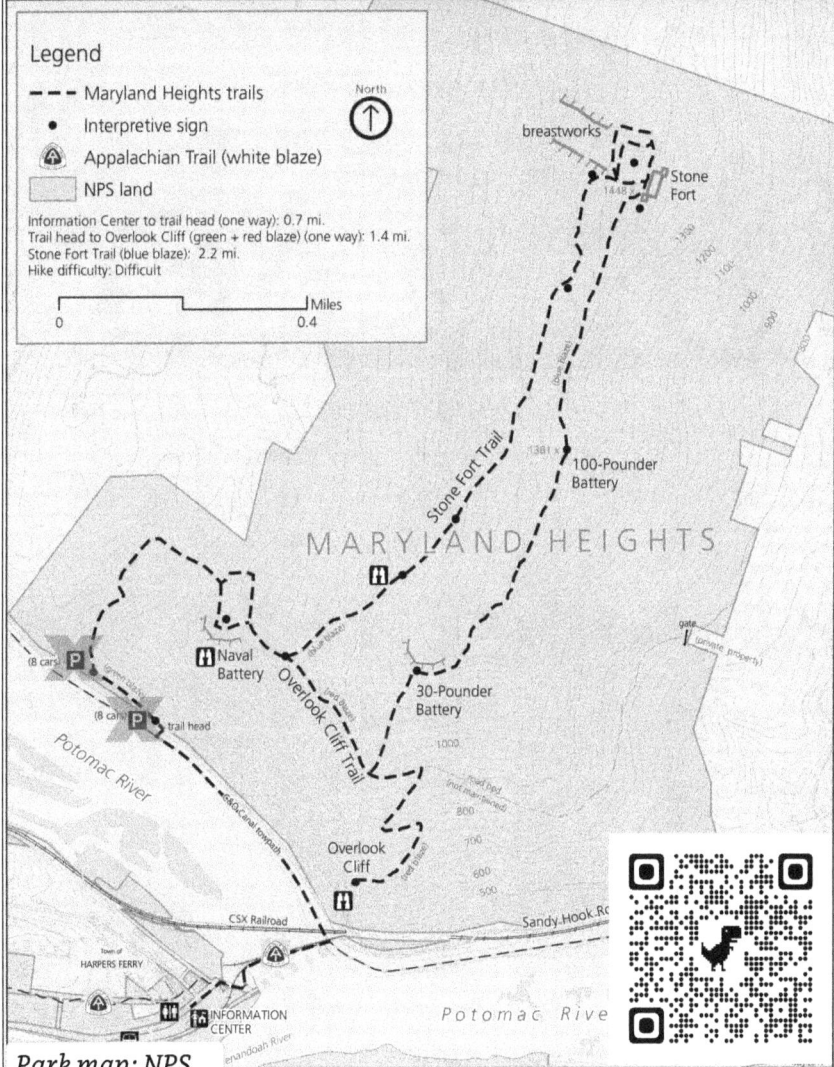

North

0   0.4   Miles

breastworks

Stone Fort

100-Pounder Battery

Stone Fort Trail

MARYLAND HEIGHTS

gate (private property)

Naval Battery

Overlook Cliff Trail

30-Pounder Battery

(8 cars) trail head

Potomac River

road bed (not maintained)

Overlook Cliff

CSX Railroad

Sandy Hook Rd.

Potomac River

Town of HARPERS FERRY

INFORMATION CENTER

Shenandoah River

National Park Service: Antietam National Battlefield— Bloody Lane Trail
Sharpsburg, Maryland
Washington County

Bloody Lane

Bloody Lane, center.

Fought along the farmland around Antietam Creek near Sharpsburg, the Battle of Antietam is considered one of the Civil War's bloodiest battles. On September 17th, 1862, General Robert E. Lee and General George McClellan came face to face at the first battle on northern soil. Four hours of intense fighting occurred on an old sunken road between two farms. Confederate soldiers retreated, but not before bodies piled up in agonizing numbers in that road. Over 3,675 men lost their lives.

Bloody Lane on the right wing, where a large number of soldiers were killed at the Battle of Antietam. Image: Library of Congress.

It is humbling to walk the dirt path called Bloody Lane, knowing how many died there, who gave their lives for others' freedom. Because this was one big decisive battle—it allowed President Lincoln to issue the Emancipation Proclamation on January 1st, 1863, which freed the slaves still held in the South. The proclamation declared: "that all persons held as slaves" within the rebellious states "are, and henceforward shall be free." It is not surprising, in the least, to hear that people have seen the ghostly apparitions of soldiers walking the fields nearby the battlefield. The scent of ghostly gunpowder wafts to nostrils, and a blue ball of light flashes across the old fields. There is a certain heavy energy in the air following those who stroll the trails.

McDonogh School in Owings Mills is a private school in Maryland. On September 17th, 1982, a class from the school took a field trip to mark the 120th anniversary of the battle. A part of their assignment during the trip was, at sunset, to walk the path of Bloody Lane with eyes closed and lay down to take in the magnitude of the battle story told to them ahead of time by two teachers dressed in soldier's uniforms.

The students did as instructed, but the two teachers decided to play a cruel prank on the kids and run through the field with blankets to frighten them during the lesson. Their joke came to an abrupt halt when one of the teachers was caught in barbed wire partway to the children and moaned loudly in pain. Some of the students heard the sound and were terrified, believing it was a dead soldier rising and began to scream.

As the teachers detached the wire and made their way to the students to calm them and let them know they were only playing a practical joke, they were the ones who were shocked. Some of the students had actually seen a ghostly riderless horse jumping over them while they lay there! Several students were sure they heard what sounded like men belting out the Christmas song Deck the Halls, the particular words "Fa-la-la-la-la, la-la-la-la" filling the air, but later believed to be a spectral battle cry of the long-dead soldiers of the Irish Brigade yelling out "Faugh A Ballagh," meaning "Clear the way!"

Years ago, a group of Civil War reenactors decided to set up camp along Bloody Lane. After they had laid down for sleep, they began to hear low moans and groans sometime during the night. Unsettled, each individually made their way back to their cars to finish out the night until one lone reenactor remained behind. Suddenly, a scream filled the air, and the men in their vehicles jumped out to find the only man left behind rushing from the camp thoroughly shaken. When the reenactor could finally catch his breath, he told the men that while he lay there half-awake, he had seen a hand and arm raise from the earth beneath him, slide across his chest and pull him as if to drag him down into the packed dirt. When he screamed, the hand and arm vanished!

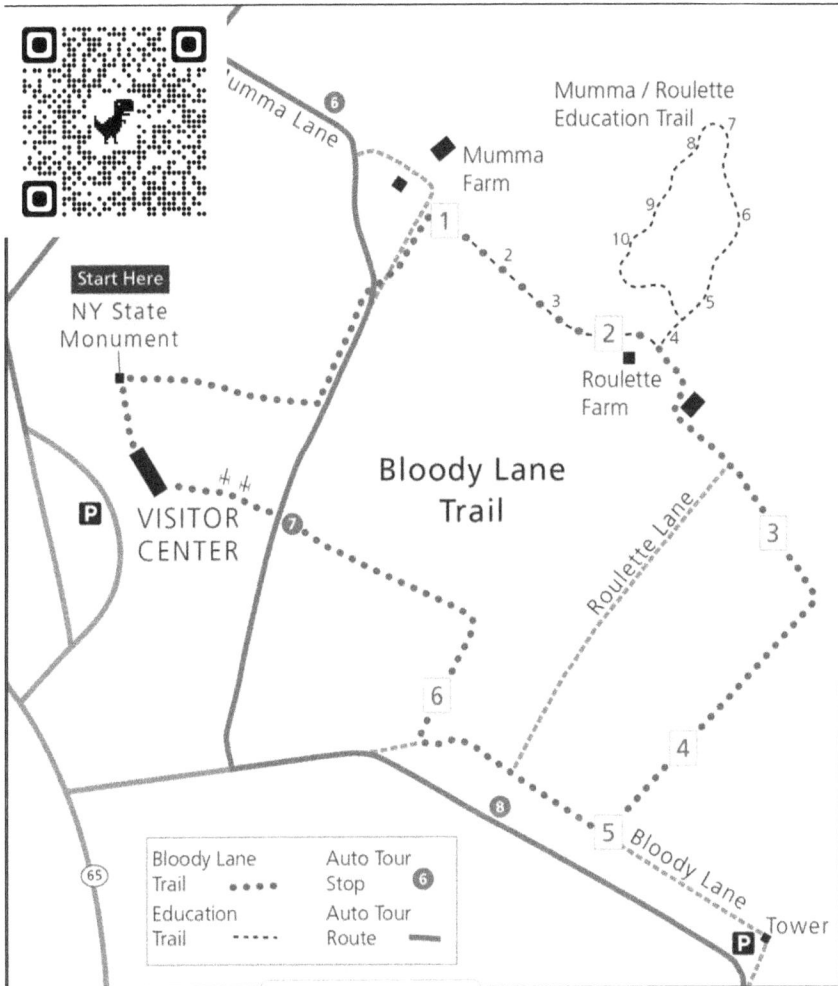

Park map: NPS

That National Park Service has an interactive map on their website under: Plan Your Visit/Maps

Parking/Trailhead: Antietam National Battlefield
Battle of Antietam
5831 Dunker Church Road
Sharpsburg, MD 21782
(39.470737, -77.739818)

Trail: 1.6 miles. The Bloody Lane Trail is located at the Antietam National Battlefield. It begins at the New York State Monument. It ends near the cannon behind the NPS visitor center.

Along the Appalachian Trail in the South Mountain

In Maryland, South Mountain stretches southward from the Pennsylvania border to the Potomac River. Within its grasp are forests, farmland, small towns, and the Appalachian Trail. And along the Appalachian Trail, in about a 3-mile section peculiarly prevailing with haunts, there are a few spine-tingling stories that stand out amongst the rest—

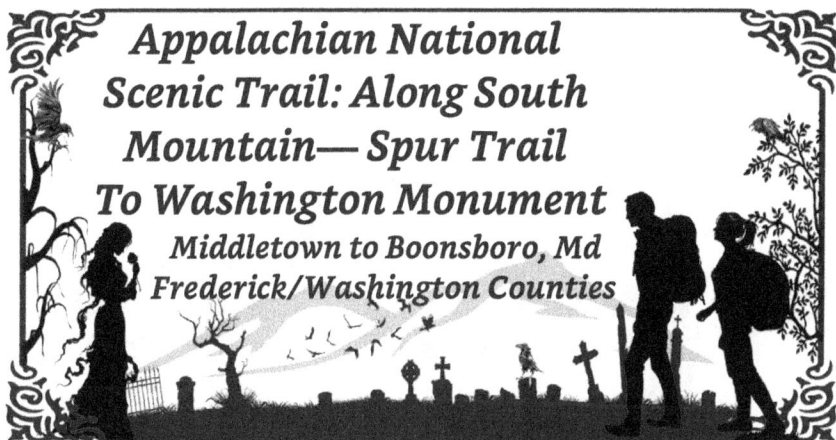

Appalachian National Scenic Trail: Along South Mountain— Spur Trail To Washington Monument
Middletown to Boonsboro, Md Frederick/Washington Counties

Buried Alive

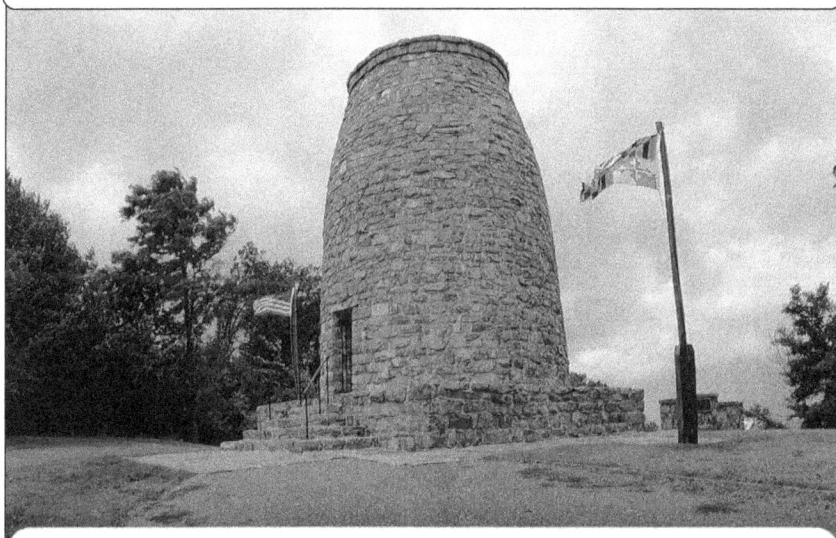

The Washington Monument is just a short jog off the Appalachian trail—I started the short walk up and a tree-bending, lightning-wielding thunderstorm rolled through. I was quickly shooed away by a park ranger as rain pelted down and thick, eerie fog crept up the trail. I was glad she did. I found out later that occasionally, the tower gets struck by lightning!

The rugged stone tower of Washington Monument is along the Appalachian Trail near the summit of South Mountain's Monument Knob. It has fallen into disrepair several times and rebuilt since its original creation in 1827.

The trail to Washington Monument—

A local legend recalls a cave system found among the rocky crag below the monument. When the Civil War raged nearby, a young soldier stopped at a nearby farm for water from its well. There he met and fell in love with the landowner's beautiful daughter. The young woman talked the soldier into deserting the army so that they could run away together, and they hid in the caves beneath the monument, waiting for the battle to push forward and away from the area. Then they would escape and elope. But during one harrowing night, while the war raged close, a rockfall buried the two lovers alive, cutting off the entrance. For days, they tried to free themselves, screaming and crying for help, to no avail. Today, those hiking to the monument have heard the distressing cries of the dead within as they still desperately try to get free.

Appalachian National Scenic Trail:
Along South Mountain—
Old South Mountain Inn
Middletown to Boonsboro, Md
Frederick/Washington Counties

Mysterious Happenings Near the Old South Mountain Inn

As dusk and a storm settle in around Old South Mountain Inn where the Appalachian Trail passes by, it is not difficult to imagine its ghosts strolling about the property—

One of those old byways, the National Pike, forges through at Turner's Gap (a wind gap in the South Mountain Range) near Boonsboro. At the top, a flourishing 21-room tavern/inn was built in the late 1700s by Robert Turner.

The property was sold in 1876 to Madeleine Dahlgren, a wealthy widow, and turned into a private residence. Then, in the 1920s, it became a tavern again. Over the years, it became a welcome stopping point for travelers taking the climb to the top—waggoneers, stagecoach drivers, teamsters, and tourists. It is now Old South Mountain Inn.

Over the years that Dahlgren owned the home, there were mysterious happenings both inside and outdoors. When looking out the windows at night, guests staying within the house saw strange lights and glowing apparitions floating on the grounds. Most believed it was the remnants of dead soldiers who had fought nearby during the Civil War. Others speculated it was a man murdered in the inn's early years, a traveler who stopped at the inn, disappeared from his room, and whose decomposed body was discovered not far from the lodgings.

There was once a spring along the road near here where a ghostly dog would tarry before making its way toward the South Mountain Inn—

It is also here along the mountain that the story of the Snarly Yow began. As nightfall would set over the sprinkling of rural cabins and homes on the side of South Mountain, this shadowy dog would slip from wherever its hiding place was in the forest during the daylight. It took the same narrow path until it crossed the dirt road. There, it continued down until it came to a small and meandering stream where it would disappear.

If the beast would not have been monstrous in size and had minded its own business, locals would have probably mistaken it for a farmer's wandering dog. But it had a strangeness about it as a thirty-year-old local family man named William would attest in the late 1800s. One evening around ten o'clock, the strapping farmer was returning from the store in Boonsboro. It was a clear night, and the road was easy to see. But just as William reached a particular part of the trail, a huge black dog appeared from the brush and would not allow the man to pass. William pushed forward as if to go around, but the dog grew in length enough to cover the entire road from one side to the other! Its mouth grinned at him, disturbingly wide and bloody red. Undaunted, William rushed at the creature, arm whipping downward to beat it back, but his fists met no resistance and struck the air. The dog bit and clawed back. Again and again, William fought the dog. Then just as quickly as it had appeared, it disappeared. Later, upon holding up his arms, William saw no bruises or cuts. He was utterly unharmed, barring the emotional toll the battle had left on him.

Others have come into contact with the Snarly Yow and not just along the National Pike cutting through the South Mountain. Hikers have seen it along the Appalachian Trail on the mountain and near Harpers Ferry. When approached, it fades away. Not too far in the past, a couple traveling along the road in their car hit a giant black dog.

Following the path of the Snarly Yow—

After hearing the sound of bone crushing and the thud of the body underneath, they were able to stop. But when they got out of the car to look, there was no animal beneath. There was only the solitary shadow of a dog on the road behind them snarling.

Appalachian National Scenic Trail: Along South Mountain— Wise's Well

Middletown to Boonsboro, Md Frederick/Washington Counties

The Dead Men in Daniel Wise's Well

The old farmstead of Daniel Wise before it fell to ruins, and where unsettled ghostly soldiers were hard to lay to rest.

The Battle of South Mountain was fought on September 14, 1862, as part of the Maryland campaign of the American Civil War. It was over control of several strategically important mountain passes, places large numbers of soldiers could more easily cross. Amid this bloody battle was the Daniel Wise homestead located in the center of one of those much-coveted passes—Fox's Gap. The property and fields he and his two children used to sustain their farm were used as a battlefield, hospital, and burial ground.

In the end, the Union Army prevailed. That left the occupying Union soldiers in charge of burials. The soil was so hard and rocky in the area that the men had a difficult time digging graves for the dead. So much so that they could shovel less than a foot and a half down, leaving fingers and toes sticking out of the earth. As it happened, Daniel Wise's property had a deep well.

A soldier of the 12th Ohio volunteer infantry Samuel W. Compton witnessed the burial as such:

"On the morning of the 16th, I strolled out to see them bury the Confederate dead. I saw but I never want to [see] another [such] sight. The squad I saw were armed with pick and canteen full of whiskey, the whiskey the most necessary of the two. The bodies had become so offensive that the men could only endure it by being staggering drunk. To see men stagger up to corpses and strike four or five times before they could get ahold, a right hold being one above the belt. Then staggering, as every drunk will, they dragged the corpses to a 60-foot well and tumbled them in. What a sepulcher and what a burial! You don't wonder why I had no appetite for supper!"

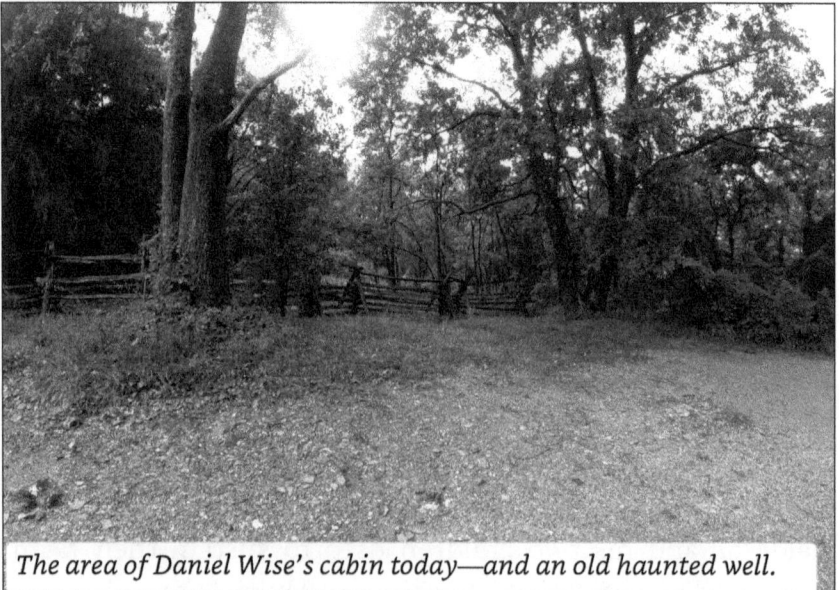

The area of Daniel Wise's cabin today—and an old haunted well.

Later, Daniel Wise was compensated a dollar a body (most likely for tainting his well), and years later, the bodies were moved to the Confederate Cemetery in Hagerstown and reburied.

During the time between the return of the Wise family to their farm along Old Sharpsburg Road (now Reno Monument Road) and the reburials of the soldiers in the well, a ghostly soldier returned to haunt Daniel. Each night, he was awakened by a soldier above his bed telling him that he was in an uncomfortable position and could not rest eternally if his body was not buried properly. Even now, hikers passing the old homestead area along the Appalachian Trail, where there is a small parking area, have witnessed a thudding noise—the ghostly sound of the soldiers' bodies being dumped into the well.

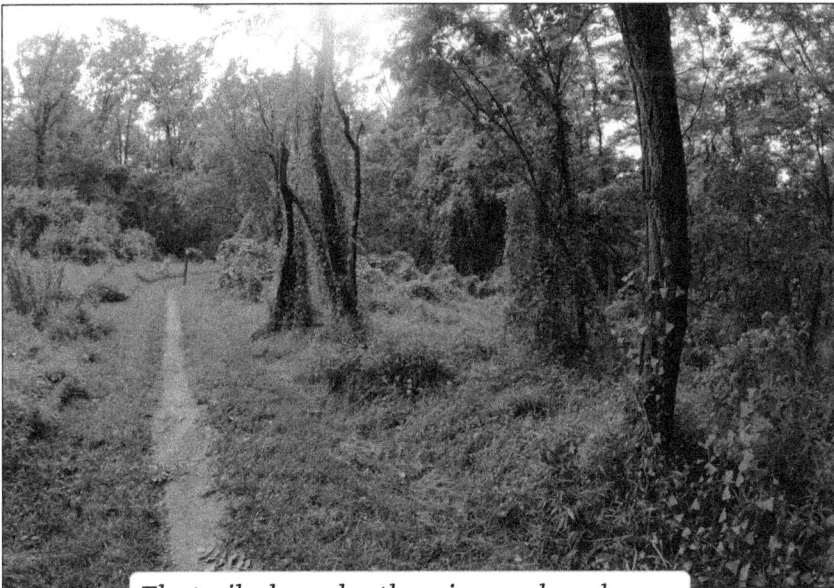

The trail where ghostly noises are heard—

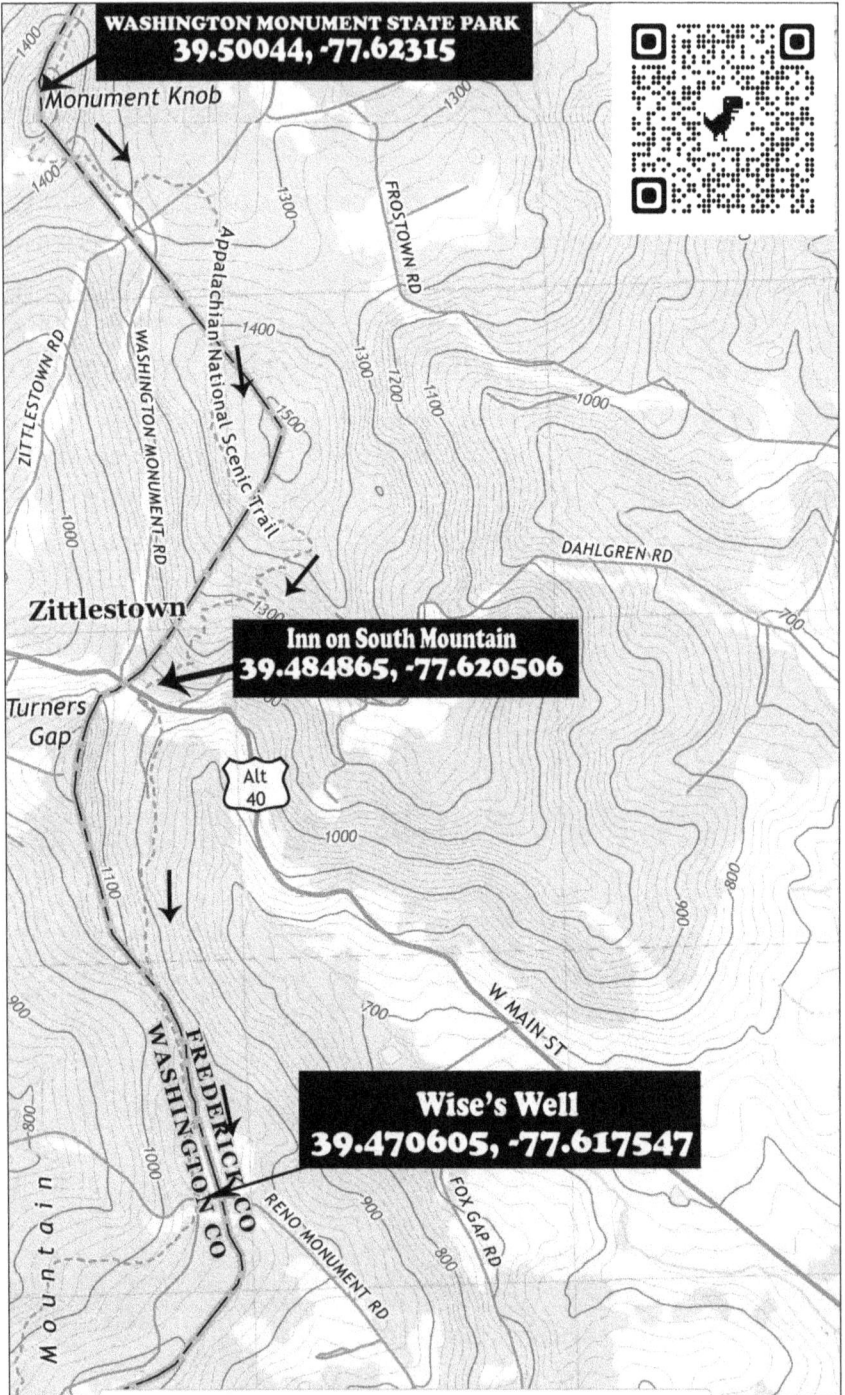

WASHINGTON MONUMENT STATE PARK
39.50044, -77.62315

Monument Knob

FROSTOWN RD

Appalachian National Scenic Trail

ZITTLESTOWN RD

WASHINGTON MONUMENT RD

DAHLGREN RD

Zittlestown

Inn on South Mountain
39.484865, -77.620506

Turners Gap

Alt 40

W MAIN ST

FREDERICK CO
WASHINGTON CO

Wise's Well
39.470605, -77.617547

RENO MONUMENT RD

FOX GAP RD

Mountain

Map: Open Street Maps/USGS topographic maps.

Park/Trail: Begin at Washington Monument and hike the Appalachian Trail just shy of 3.0 miles (one-way) along to Wise's Well with a stop partway to view Old South Mountain Inn and perhaps see a ghost and look for the Snarly Yow. Out and back. Part of the trail is marked with interpretive signs.

Washington Monument State Park
6620 Zittlestown Road
Boonsboro, MD 21713 (39.50044, -77.62315)

Inn on South Mountain
6137-6199 US-40 ALT
Boonsboro, MD 21713 (39.484865, -77.620506)

Wise's Well
Appalachian National Scenic Trail
Maryland (39.470605, -77.617547)

I feel I would be remiss if I did not mention the legend that comes with Gapland Road heading into Burkittsville after passing Mountain Church Road—called Spook Hill. During the Civil War and at night as Confederates headed for the Battle of Cramptons Gap, their soldiers heaved cannons up the hill in darkness to conceal their moves in preparation for battle. However, they were discovered by Union soldiers and fled, leaving their cannons to roll back down the hill. Cars moving slowly or in neutral here will get a push up the hill by the ghostly hands of those long-dead Confederate soldiers. Of course, when there was no traffic, my daughter and I tried it and it works. Remember, this is a public road so use caution and hazard flashers. Try at your own risk. (39.396893, -77.634492)Is it an elaborate optical illusion caused by the lay of the land or a ghost? Hmm. You decide.

Pennsylvania

Great Allegheny Passage Rail-Trail

The Great Allegheny Passage offers 150 miles of hiking and biking trail from Cumberland, Maryland to Pittsburgh, Pennsylvania. Along its route, it passes many old towns and abandoned communities. Among them, a few have gotten quite a reputation as being haunted. And those who dare, can visit them.

Dead Man's Hollow
Conservation Area—
Great Allegheny Passage
McKeesport, Pennsylvania
Allegheny County

Dead Man's Hollow

For those who like to explore abandoned places and old souls left behind, the Great Allegheny Passage trail leads to both historic remains of the land's eventful past and its ghosts at Dead Man's Hollow about a half hour from Pittsburgh.

The Youghiogheny River winds its way from the Backbone Mountain along the border of Maryland and West Virginia and northward 132 miles. It eventually joins the Monongahela River near McKeesport, Pennsylvania. Along its way and just three miles from this union is a dark forest valley known for its grim legends and surly ghosts. It is called Dead Man's Hollow, and its name has long been explained like this—

Many corpses have shown up along the banks of the Youghiogheny River at this point. It is the perfect dumping site as the river is bent and twisted at an ideal angle here to catch the dead. When the water flows past, anything with weight bobbing within the river's fickle grasp tends to work its way toward the shore and get stuck in the more stagnant water of the bank where a fairly small creek sweeps into it. Those who drown upriver wash up on the shore there.

One day in the 1870s, while exploring a creek valley there, a group of boys discovered a dead body hanging within the hollow. The corpse was so decomposed nobody could identify it. After, locals began identifying it as "the hollow the dead man showed up." Eventually, the name was shortened to Dead Man's Hollow. The creek running through it was dubbed Dead Man's Run.

Dead Man's Run within Dead Man's Hollow.

The Great Allegheny Passage Youghiogheny River Trail passes by this area that is now the Dead Man's Hollow Conservation Area. It is a forested pocket, quiet and serene.

But the place was not always so peaceful. There are the skeletal ruins of old buildings amid the underbrush and beside a creek, along with scraps and discards leftover from days long gone. Those bits and pieces of yesteryears—bricks and clay pipes and occasional bottles—leave clues of the area's past. Over the years, the property has changed hands. It was once a part of the 1881 George Flemming Stone Quarry, where laborers mined the rock for railroad ballast. Evidence of that quarry is still seen today in old wagon trails and sandstone, shale, and limestone rock outcroppings with holes drilled for blasting.

Union Sewer Pipe Company once at Dead Man's Hollow. Image: McKeesport Regional History & Heritage Center, McKeesport, PA

In 1893, the Union Brick & Stone Company purchased the quarry property before selling it in 1898 for use as the Bowman Brick Factory for making bricks and paving blocks. Along with foundations of kilns, their castoffs lie in the dirt and brush easily seen by a keen eye, especially the deep red-orange bricks peeking from the soil. Into the 1920s and for over 30 years, the Union Sewer Pipe Company made sewer pipe, terra cotta, building block, and fire brick and sent them by rail to many cities throughout the U.S.

By then, the area was full of brick machinery, storage buildings, elevators, stone crushers, coal-fired kilns, and derricks, some still present today. You can see parts of the old buildings used and find remnants of the terra cotta pipes knee-deep in the creek. Around 1925, there was an explosion in one of the kilns, and the business shut down. But among the scraps, thick underbrush, and building carcasses, there are a few leftovers from yesteryears that stick out the most in Dead Man's Hollow—and those are its ghosts.

Dead Man's Run—the creek running through it is an archeologist's paradise of relics of its past—whiskey bottles, old bricks, and pipe.

Thirty-five-year-old George McClure was a father of three and co-owner of Hendrickson and McClure's hardware store in the 1880s. In August of 1881, A gang of thieves, including 19-year-old ne'er-do-well thief Ward McConkey, burglarized the store. McClure, dead set on retrieving the few hundred dollars' worth of stolen goods, set out with George Flemming, who owned the property and believed he knew where the robbers had stashed loot, and another man, Joseph Lynch.

The three men searched the hollow all day and could not find any sign of the money. Finally, they stopped to rest at dusk when seven men surrounded them and began to fire. Flemming and Lynch escaped. McClure was found dead around 9:30 p.m., riddled with bullet holes, in the woods at Dead Man's Hollow.

A judge sentenced Ward McConkey to hang on May 1883 for the murder. He claimed innocence to the moment of death. The newspapers reported the 19-year-old declared these words before he died: "All I have to say, gentlemen, is that you hang me because you think I know something about the murder of George McClure and won't squeal and the people of McKeesport want to see me hanged, but I'm innocent." A white cap was placed over his face, and just before the trap was sprung, McConkey uttered, "Goodbye, murderers, goodbye." Yet his farewells were as short-lived as his brief life. To this day, if you visit the dark interior of Dead Man's Hollow, you might run into McConkey's ghost. He wanders its dim trails, a churlish spirit apt to slinking around trunks of old trees and beneath their shaded canopies. Sometimes, he slips from the shadows, a silhouette darker than the landscape behind him. "Goodbye, murderers, goodbye," he whispers as he fades away.

Relics of days gone by—Bowman Brickyard and Union Sewer Pipe Company.

In March of 1883, Foreman George Henninger, his brother, Daniel, and two other men were preparing for blasting work in the quarry. As they started to organize for the day, one of them noted that the dynamite they would be using had been frozen solid. Despite the setback, one man decided to start a small fire to thaw out a cartridge of the frozen dynamite. George Henninger and Daniel Henninger buddied up to the fire to warm their hands at about the same time that the cartridge exploded. The blast killed at least two men in what one news reporter described as "arms and legs being burned and hurled hither and thither." Passersby along the trails have witnessed the spirits of these unfortunate men. Dismembered and mangled, they hobble, totter, and crawl about on the forest floor, searching for the arms and legs they lost. A bit of breeze usually wafts past, and they dwindle away with it, followed by the stench of burnt flesh.

The Youghiogheny River and the trail to Dead Man's Hollow.

In 1887, 74-year-old Edward Woods drowned in the Youghiogheny River while riding the McClure Ferry. He lost his footing and toppled over the side of the boat, drowning.

Then in May of 1944, a married couple and a couple who were to be betrothed were returning to their home in Dead Man's Hollow via a small rowboat on the Youghiogheny. Because it was overloaded, one of the men was swimming alongside the boat. Midstream, a gust of wind before an oncoming storm overturned the vessel. The three within spilled into the depths of the river. The two women, one 33-years-old and the other only 20-years-old drowned. Those doomed to drown there seem to want company. Some have felt mysterious, ghostly hands pulling them toward the water when walking near the riverbank.

Ruins of the old industries, including Union Sewer Pipe Company, where many worked and some died.

Others have found their death within the confines of the hollow. On September 25, 1905, Mike Sacco, employed at Union Sewer Pipe Company, was leaving work. He stepped inside the elevator and tugged on the rope to lower it. Instead, it began to rise, and the worker made the rash decision to jump off. Unfortunately, he was not quick enough. Sacco's body wedged between the second-floor ceiling and the elevator floor, which crushed him to death.

In December of 1916, two hunters, following the baying of a hound they believed had tracked a rabbit, found the corpse of 40-year-old Samuel Candy of Braddock partially submerged in a creek in Dead Man's Hollow. Candy had disappeared the previous Tuesday after leaving work from the Edgar Thomson Steel Works. In a postmortem exam, Dr. Porter of McKeesport found bullets in the small of the man's back, one in the neck, one on his left side, one in the right shoulder, one in the breast, and one under the right arm. The Pittsburgh Post-Gazette made this statement: *Mr. Candy had interpreted many cases at the Braddock Police Station, and the police believe that he was the victim of enemies who thought he was betraying them to the authorities. A second motive may have been love. Candy was courting a woman from Wilmerding when another suitor came along and began threatening him "with violence."* Those, like these men, who died gruesome deaths within the threshold of Dead Man's Hollow have left their mark on the land. Ghostly chatter and ghastly screams fill the air occasionally, startling hikers.

A most intriguing story comes from a 1934 sighting by Michael Bendzuch Jr., a resident of Dead Man's Hollow, one moon-lit night. While Bendzuch crossed the Youghiogheny on a rowboat, he watched in wonder as a thin layer of fog began to float across the riverbank. Then, a silhouette favoring an Indian swept from the mist and stopped to stand along the shore, seemingly as interested in the young man on the boat as the young man was curious about the eerie presence. They both stared across the water for what seemed like an eternity before the old ghost stories told to him as a young child flittered past Bendzuch's mind. Then, quickly, he gave the shoreline a wide berth just as the mist and the ghost vanished.

The Allegheny Land Trust is now overseeing this unique piece of history, land, and the legends that come with it. These caretakers have embraced the natural beauty and its celebrated past, opening it up for everyone to explore. Those discovering its ghostly side will not be disappointed. Witnesses have heard a baby's sob within on full-moon nights, crying for whoever was murdered by the hanging in the hollow.

There is parking and trail access to the Dead Man's Hollow Conservation Area available within a short 1-mile (one-way out and back) hike along the Great Allegheny Passage Youghiogheny River Trail (rail-trail). After reaching Dead Man's Hollow, there are 8 miles of wooded trails within the hollow, including the ruins of the old buildings.

Parking: There is free parking at Boston Ballfield Park; there are several parking lots together.
Lot 1: It is seasonally suggested to park under the bridge on Donner Street (40.311470, -79.827682) to avoid broken windshields from foul balls at the fields.)
Lot 2: 1906 Donner Street
McKeesport, PA 15135
(40.310503, -79.830441)

Great Allegheny Passage Trailhead to Dead Man's Hollow:
Hike to Dead Man's Hollow—1-mile (one-way) multi-use trail (hike/bike) from parking area. Out and back. Rail-trail. Nature trail signs. Mostly flat to the hollow, after there are different level developed trails and terrain. It is wheelchair accessible (pea-gravel) to the conservation area. Trails within the hollow are not wheelchair accessible.
(40.310802, -79.828083)

Trailhead to Trails within Dead Man's Hollow:
Great Allegheny Passage (North)
McKeesport, PA 15135
(40.317985, -79.840733)

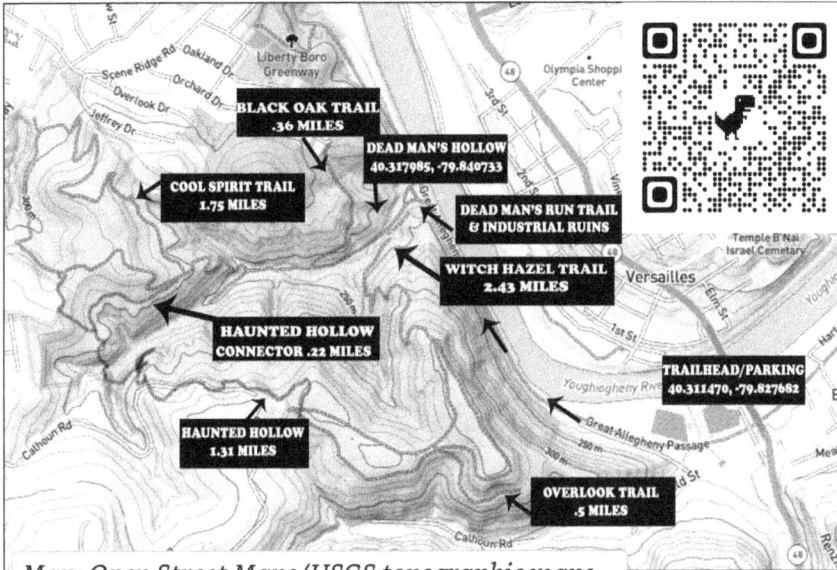

Map: Open Street Maps/USGS topographic maps.

The trailhead to Dead Man's Hollow: *1-mile, one-way. Out and back.*
Trails within Dead Man's Hollow*:

- *Cool Spirit Trail: 1.75 (Loop)*
- *Dead Man's Run Trail: (Along Creek)*
- *Overlook Trail: 0.50 (Loop)*
- *Haunted Hollow: 1.31 (Out and back and Connects to Loops)*
- *Witch Hazel Trail: 2.43 miles (Loop)*
- *Black Oak Trail: 0.36 miles (Spur)*
- *Overlook Trail: 1.5 miles (Spur from Witch Hazel loop trail)*

Enchanted Staircase on the Witch Hazel Trail—

Dravo Cemetery at North Buena Vista Historical Park— Great Allegheny Passage
Buena Vista, Pennsylvania
Allegheny County

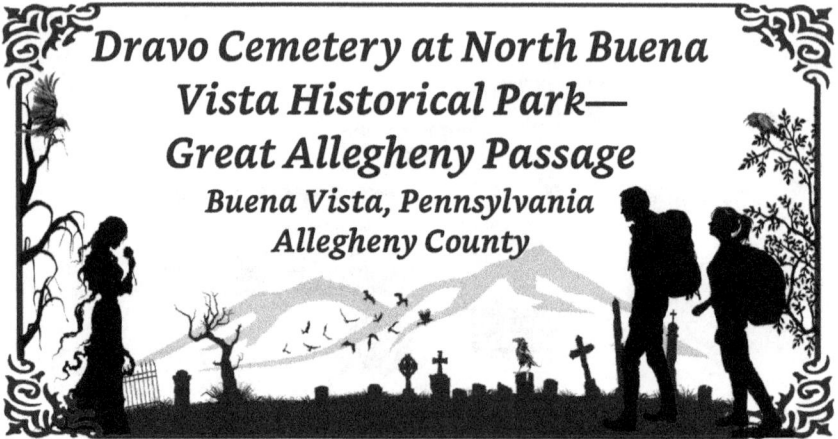

Two-headed Dog and a Ghost Train

Haunted rail-trail train tracks to the left passing the haunted Dravo Cemetery to the right—Hikers and bikers can find a good scare along the Great Allegheny Passage.

A two-headed dog haunts an old graveyard along an isolated railroad track. Although no one living can explain the cause of the dog's appearance, some believe two-headed creatures can see into this world and the world of the dead.

The cemetery itself is like any other almost lost to time and natural elements. It is an old one dating back to when William Newlin, an early farmer in the late 1700s, set aside a grassy hillock overlooking the river for a quiet location to use as a family burial ground. It was not long after and in the mid-1800s that coal mining towns began to pop up nearby, including nearby Stringtown—so named for the string or series of homes along the roadway.

Dravo Cemetery today. Center and to the left of the large tree is the area where the church once stood.

As the area grew, so too did the population. Noting that the community needed a place of worship, Reverend William Dravo, who was close friends with the Newlin family, sought permission to erect a church on their property. Approval was granted, and churchgoers built a two-story Methodist Church next to the family cemetery in 1824. In addition, they expanded the burial plot to also take in the community's dead.

By 1882, the Pittsburgh and Lake Erie Railroad had developed a line along the Youghiogheny River and through the little hamlet as it made its way from Pittsburgh through Connellsville. After, the surrounding communities and their church members would grow along with the number of graves in the cemetery. And the church would probably still be here today, a lone memorial for the towns that once stood, except the building burned down twice before folks realized sparks from the trains passing close by started the fires. The parishioners never rebuilt the second time. By the 1930s, the industries in the area began to wane, and the cemetery was so overgrown the graves were hardly noticeable.

The trail— Great Allegheny Passage and the Youghiogheny River .

Now, all that remains of the long-gone coal town along the river, barring the trail, modern public restroom, picnic shelter, and campsite—are the stones of those buried there. They were gently restored during the 1990s by a scout group. But as the cemetery became more accessible to hikers and bikers, witnesses began seeing a two-headed dog lurking about the graveyard.

The first reported sighting was from a group of scouts who had gotten permission to camp near the old graveyard one night. While on a light-hearted foray to check for ghosts at the cemetery, howls burst into the air in the darkness of night, and the boys hurried back to the camp with fearful excitement, daring to divulge they had seen a two-headed dog with red eyes bounding from behind one of the headstones. Others testify seeing the strange dog. It appears and disappears or leaves a mournful cry echoing through the hills. Those biking past have also witnessed shadows standing near the graves. A few visitors to the area also claim to feel a rush of wind along the tracks, hear the grind of steel wheels on the rail, and see the eerie outline of a ghost train looming in the distance.

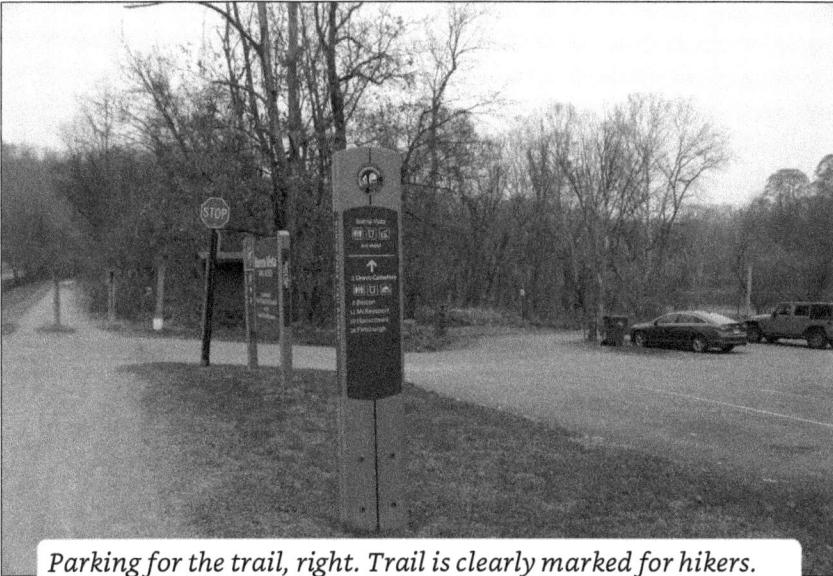

Parking for the trail, right. Trail is clearly marked for hikers.

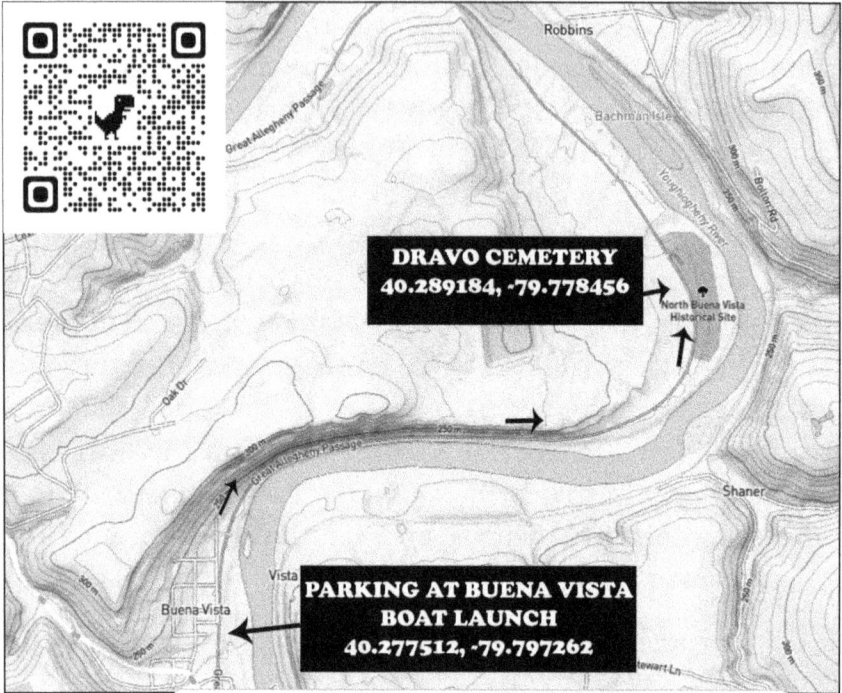

Map: Open Street Maps/USGS topographic maps.

Parking:
Parking lot is located at the intersection of Wood and McGowan streets at the boat launch.
Buena Vista Public Boat Launch
Sutersville, PA 15083
(40.277512, -79.797262)

Trail: Hike to Dravo Cemetery—1.7 miles (one-way) Flat surface. Multi-use (hike/bike). Out and back. Rail-trail.
(40.289184, -79.778456)
Some maps show Henderson Road open to the cemetery, but it cannot be accessed here.

Presque Isle State Park

Presque Isle State Park is a sandy peninsula arching out into Lake Erie in Erie, Pennsylvania. Although it is known by most as a summer vacation destination, it has a ghostly past and an eerie mariner legend.

Presque Isle State Park—
Graveyard Pond Trail
Erie, Pennsylvania
Erie County

Dead Soldiers of the War of 1812

During the War of 1812, 27-year-old Commodore Oliver Hazard Perry was sent to the Northwest Frontier, particularly the area of Presque Isle, to build and command a fleet for the United States in their battles against Great Britain which was restricting American trade. The hope of the U.S. was to take control of Lake Erie. The isle provided protection during the building of the ships.

Despite the lack of materials and workers, many of whom had fled for fear of raids, he was able to assemble a makeshift fleet while the shores and waters of Presque Isle protected the ships during construction. However, during this time, when the boats were moored at Little Bay on the island, the men of the fleet began getting symptoms of severe diarrhea, vomiting, and dehydration, called Lake Fever, and caused by poor nutrition, close quarters, and the mixing of drinking/cooking water with human waste. It made its way quickly through Perry's camp and some men died and were buried in the shallow depths of what is called Graveyard Pond. Their ghosts have been seen trudging along the water's edge in raggedy, torn clothing.

Along the trail—

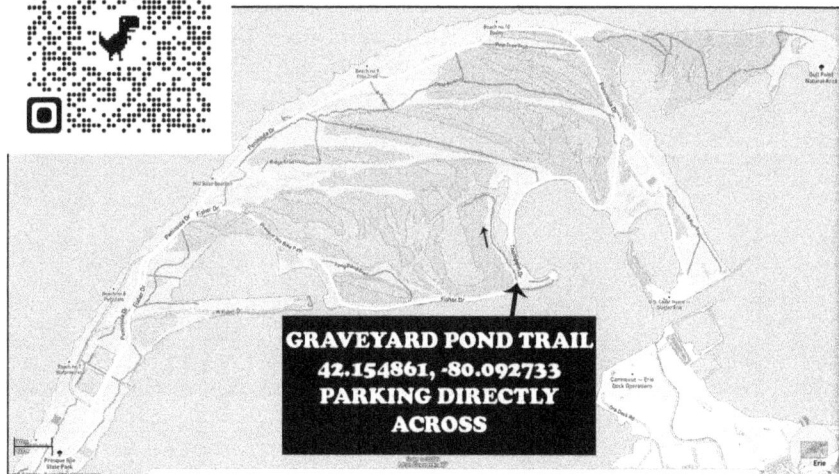

GRAVEYARD POND TRAIL
42.154861, -80.092733
PARKING DIRECTLY
ACROSS

Map: Open Street Maps/USGS topographic maps.

Parking: Directly across from the trail entrance.
Thompson Drive
Erie, PA 16507
(42.155354, -80.092143)

Trail: The trail follows the shoreline along Graveyard Pond.
0.75 miles. Out and back. Maintained. Seasonal flooding.
Trailhead: (42.154861, -80.092733)

Presque Isle State Park— Karl Boyes Multi-Purpose National Recreation Trail
Erie, Pennsylvania
Erie County

Presque Isle Storm Hag

I have witnessed storms on Presque Isle and they are beautiful and breathtaking. They are also dangerous to pedestrians and boaters. Folklore stories have long been passed down that the worst of these squalls are called up by a Storm Hag who has an insatiable appetite for human flesh.

Presque Isle State Park is a sandy peninsula arching into Lake Erie near Erie, Pennsylvania. Lake Erie is prone to erratic waves, shifting sandbars, and wild, unpredictable storms—its treacherous, shallow depths are known to harbor many a shipwreck up and down the coast.

Early explorers along the seventy-six miles of Pennsylvania's shorelines used this peninsula's eastern bay as a windbreak to beach boats during the many volatile storms. Unfortunately, not all those who sought its shelter made it out intact. The Lake Erie Quadrangle, a stretch of 2,500 square miles embracing an expansive shipwreck graveyard, holds more wrecks than the Bermuda Triangle. Presque Isle is right amid its epicenter.

An ancient legend explains the number of wrecks around Presque Isle. A ghastly green Storm Hag with pasty skin, a pointed chin, and green locks of hair lives near the peninsula at the bottom of Lake Erie. Her arms are long, and her nails sharp. Her large eyes are yellow, and her green teeth are sharply pointed like a shark. She emerges once in a while to feed upon those unfortunate sailors who come close to her lair. Before she attacks, she sings an enticing song that flows across the water. Then she calls up a ferocious storm to sink the boat and snatch up her meal. Sometimes she creeps to the land and hides in the trees waiting for little children to wander off from parents so she can stretch out her long arms and drag them to the water and drown them.

Misery Bay view: Thomson Drive Erie, PA 16507 (42.160077, -80.086220)

A traditional story of the Storm Hag's ruthlessness and Lake Erie's unpredictable squalls centers around a ship caught in a storm on Lake Erie in 1782. Seeing the black clouds rise on the horizon, the captain tried desperately to steer his ship toward Presque Isle's protective peninsula. To get to safety, he had to navigate past a dangerously shallow area before the storm hit where many boats before him had gone down, trying with the same desperation to get to the shelter of the small bay. He did not make it and watched just short of the treacherous path while the waves beat his boat viciously side to side. He dared not take the risk. Suddenly, the storm stopped, and the clouds slipped away to moonlight, shining off the calm waters. The sailors sighed, and the captain hailed a course through the shallows.

It was halfway through the dangerous shallows that they heard the soft song slipping through the breeze—the deep lulling wail wind makes passing through a nearly-closed window. *Come, lads, come. Tis safe, it is.* The men froze in utter horror as the moonlight dribbled away to darkness, and a foamy fog crept along with the clouds lurking across the sky above. The Siren. The Storm Hag. She bestowed her fury on the ship, then in one bolt of lightning and a rousing smash of thunder. The Storm Hag burst from her lair in the bowels of the lake and attacked with the storm relentlessly. Eventually, the boat disappeared with its crew in the black depths.

While walking the shoreline, you'll notice tiny white crystals on the beach. A local man told me that the crystals are made from the tears of the wives and mothers of those sailors lured to their death in the Lake Erie waters. It was believed holding one in the cup of the palm during a storm might help ward off the Storm Hag's fury.

Map: Open Street Maps/USGS topographic maps.

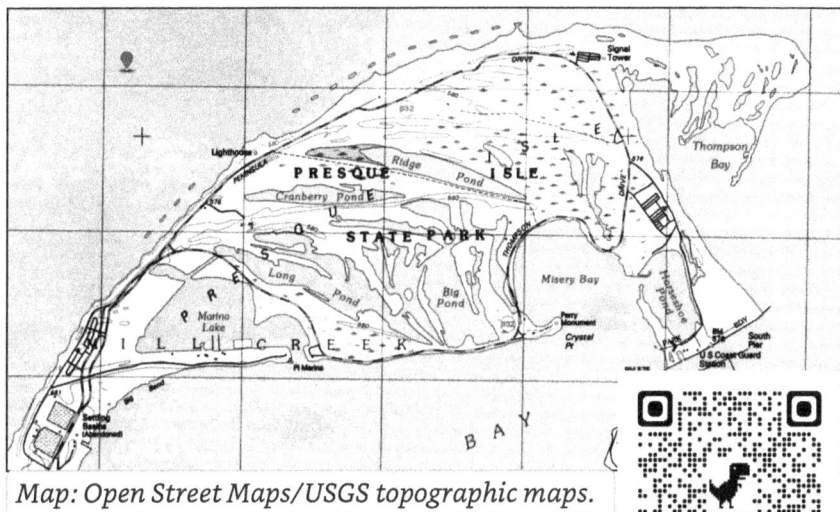

Parking: Parking lot just inside the park entrance, and ample parking throughout the park.
Parking Lot
Peninsula Drive
Erie, PA 16507
(42.123116, -80.147592)

Trail: **Hike all or part of Karl Boyes Multi-Purpose National Recreation Trail**—13.5 miles circuit where you can view the lake where the Storm Hag lives. Multi-purpose trail. Paved. This trail goes around the island, but you do not have to hike the entire route. There are many parking lots throughout where you can walk this particular trail, or hike along the beach. It is wheelchair accessible.

View of Misery Bay:

More Trails Around the Appalachian Region of Pennsylvania

Irwin Run Conservation Area—
Old Irwin Road Trail
McCandless, Pennsylvania
Allegheny County

Blue Mist Road

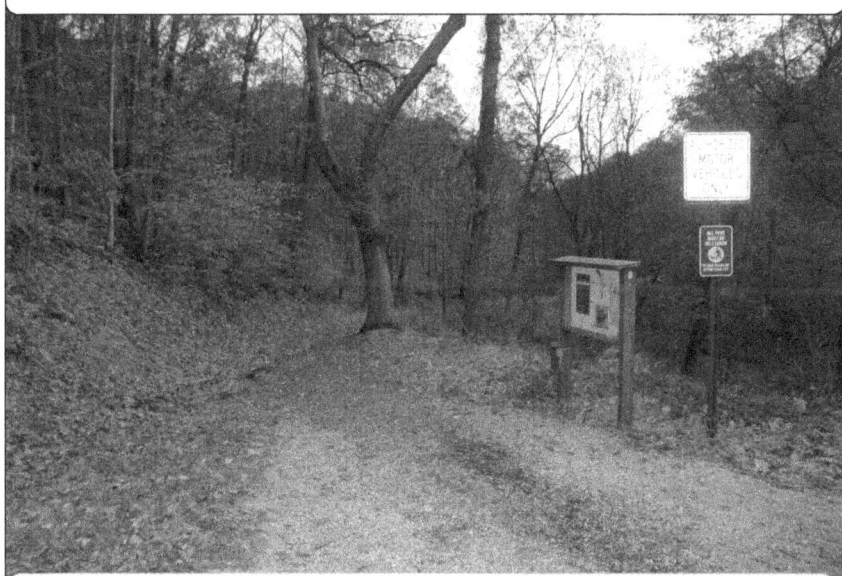

The trail near the intersection of Jackson and Irwin roads. Do not let the encouraging nature trail signs fool you—it may be an ominous journey ahead. For example, center to the image might be a hanging tree. And that's only a few steps in—

One of Pittsburgh's most haunted trails is Blue Mist Road in the North Hills. The hiking section is blocked from traffic, runs about 1.4 miles from a turnoff of Babcock Road to Jackson/Irwin Road, and offers an isolated path created from an old street running beside the sometimes-swampy Irwin Run where occasionally, a blue mist forms.

The roadway has been there since at least the early 1900s. There were once a few homes with long driveways leading to their back doors along its route. This section of Irwin Road is now blocked off and run by the Allegheny Land Trust, preserved for a hiking trail. You do not need to walk far off a little pull-off on Jackson Road, where the cold air hits the warm to get a spooky feel. The creek lets off a foggy mist that wiggles its way through a pocket of the forest and along the lonely path.

Along the old road where strange entities have been witnessed.

There are stories of dark shadows following travelers along the old roadbed. When approached, they fade away. Some might think it had gotten a bad name in the 1970s when newspapers covered a bizarre drug party and a sniper attack along Irwin Road. In March of 1970, an unidentified gunman took two shots at a policeman serving a warrant for a 19-year-old driving on a suspended license. Then on Friday, June 26, 1970, the police received a report of a man dancing naked on Irwin Road. It ended with a teenage girl getting hit by a car (she lived), a dog getting shot because it bit a policeman (it did not live), and a drug bust with minors involved.

Then there have been a few deaths—a 44-year-old man was found leaning against a tree with a gunshot wound to his head in January of 1979, his death considered a hunting mishap. And there have been a couple of wrecks near Babcock Road, one with the fatality of a mother of two young children.

When I walked the road on a dimming evening as winter started in, I had not planned on the untimely dark of night sneaking in at a mere five o'clock. It was a warmer day a week after early winter snow. The mixture caused the fog to rise along the bank at dusk, then work its way up the path. It was eerie, surreal. A Great Horned Owl was hoo-hoo-hooing in a low tone in the woods. My camera caught some insects reflecting like orbs in the LCD screen when I peeked to see what ghosts I had captured with my lens. My foggy breath had crept up into the air to look like vaporous spooks in the images I could see.

An evening walk along Blue Mist Trail with its ghostly tales leaves very little up to the imagination. Especially with my breath catching in the pictures when I would peek at them.

I began to conjure up some spooks myself. I felt somewhat uneasy walking there and quickened my steps. It is not typical. Maybe it was my imagination running wild with the pictures I was taking. I walk darkened trails all the time without feeling little more than wary of unfamiliar humans I might come upon.

But as the fog gathered me in its grasp, I could not help but recall an urban legend I had heard surrounding Blue Mist Road. Many years ago, a young couple had driven along this same secluded road before authorities blocked it for foot traffic. The two worked the car along its rugged path. They had heard the same tales I had been told—of little people who chased teen cars, of shots ringing out from a gun held in phantom hands at those who traversed the isolated road. They, too, had read of the ghostly remnants of Ku Klux Klan lynchings in this neck of the woods and a particularly ancient tree where the ghostly remains of their victims still dangled while wisps of white cloaks circled the knotted trunk. Occasionally witnesses report a half-man and half-cow lurking in the shadows and peeping through car windows at the occupants inside.

This night, the young couple was looking for the old hanging tree. Twice, they traversed the rugged, gravel-dirt road as the evening left the sky, and the hint of darkness began surrounding all but the tan-orange headlights. Finally, unable to find the tree, the two parked the car, letting it idle. They chose a secluded spot near an old driveway overgrown with tall grass leading to what they surely believed could be a buckle-roofed house—a haunted, buckle-roofed house, that is. There they sat and chatted. They watched their breath condensate on the windshield and awaited full darkness along with the mist that witnesses said would creep up around the car along with knotted-knuckled fingers patting on the roof or the glass.

"Okay, here we go—" Then, the boy turned off his car with a simple swivel of his fingers to the key and a smug twist of his lips. He swallowed hard, making a show of it, so the girl giggled. "Honk the horn three times," she told him. And so, he did. *Beep-beep-beep.*

"Now, we count to ten," the boy whispered in the silence so deathly that the pressure almost hurt his ears. "And wait for the ghosts to come."

One-two-three— When the tendrils of fog began to creep up toward the doors, the boy and girl began to count to ten. They prepared themselves to join the many legend trippers before them. They would watch the tale unfold as they started to count, go through the steps, see whatever shades of death would test their courage this night. *Four-five-six*— They counted softly together as the darkness cloaked the horizon, and quiet filled the inside of the car. It was exhilarating, this thrill. The mist crawled its way to the windshield, a bluish tone reflecting off the deep turquoise of what little remained of the evening sky. *Seven-eight-nine*—

"Ten," the girl said quietly as the darkness and fog enveloped them. "Now, see if the car starts." The boy chuckled softly and let his hand rise to the ignition. He grasped the still-warm key in his fingers, turning it with great drama, knowing it would start, but enjoying the way the girl tilted nervously forward in her seat in both panic and fascination. *Ching-ching.* But it did not start. Silence enveloped the two.

Pat-pat. Something made a soft beat on the roof. The girl's eyes widened. "It's just dew dripping from the trees," the boy said a little too quickly, flaunting his common sense even if his voice was shaky. His heart was racing, startled. Then he brushed the fear off. "Or a branch hitting it." She nodded. But his hands were trembling a bit as he struggled with the key once again. *Ching-ching.*

The boy wrestled momentarily with the ghost stories he had heard lurking about of vengeful witches, a demon-liked creature half-man and half-cow, and angry ghosts prowling around outside. Still, he decided he would rather battle any wicked creature than deal with the wrath of the girl's father if she were late getting home tonight. He would have to explain why his car broke down on secluded Irwin Road. Surely, it was just frayed wires wet from the muddy road and the tendrils of fog creeping up from the creek and under the hood. He told the girl the tapping was just a branch banging on the roof, opened the door, and stepped out into the darkness. She watched the fog envelop him as soon as he closed the door. The boy disappeared into the mist. She jumped, startled at the boom when he unlatched the hood, and the hinges made a squeaky opening. Then it was silent again.

Pat-pat. She listened to the boy poking around beneath the hood, working his way upward in the engine to find a frayed wire or a busted hose. *Tap-tap.* The girl sat back in the seat, trying not to listen to her heart pounding as it kept rhythm to the taps coming from the roof again. *Tap-tap.*

Time seemed to pass and sluggishly—too slowly for the girl. Had it been five minutes? Or ten? *Tap-tap.* She unrolled the window just a bit and called out the boy's name. Only silence returned. *Tap-tap.* The sound on the roof of the car unnerved her, and she quickly rolled up the window with wide eyes, peering upward as if she could see something through the vinyl and metal.

Tap-tap. Now the noise was more irritating than scary. Surely the boy was standing with a stick in his hand, stabbing it at the roof, waiting in the mist, waiting for her to come outside so he could jump out and scare her. "Stop it!" she yelled at the hood, then the window, then the roof. "It isn't funny." *Tap-tap.* But he did not come out.

Finally, the girl pushed open the car door and stomped along the muddy ground in a fit of rage. She waggled her head, searching for the stick, and instead found her eyes catching on something white dangling just above the roof, almost hidden in the mist. *Tap-tap.* She narrowed her eyes and leaned forward, peering hard into the haze. She pulled up a hand slowly, reluctantly reached out, and poked the white thing with the tip of her forefinger. It was warm and appeared to bob away. The mist parted lazily by her hand, and she squinted where her fingers still lay suspended next to the thing she had touched. *Was it—the grubby toe of a tennis shoe?* To her horror, she could see the pointed toe of a tennis shoe barely touching the roof of the car. *Tap-tap.* She followed it up to a blue-jeaned leg, and then as a bit of mist parted, the boy dangling there with a noose around his neck. The wind wiggled the branch on the tree, and his toe hit the roof. *Tap-tap. Tap-tap—*

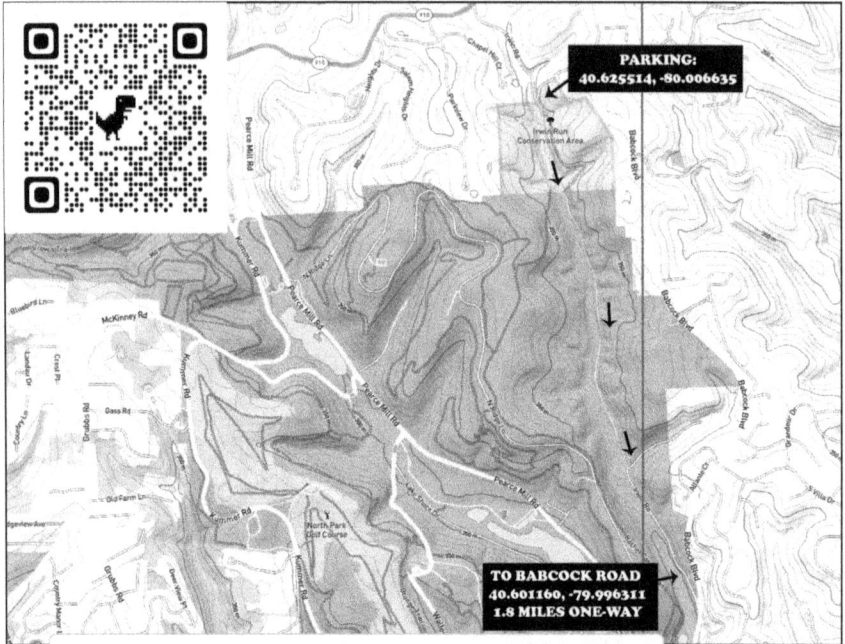

Map: Open Street Maps/USGS topographic maps.

Parking: There is a small parking area at Irwin Road
425 Irwin Road
Gibsonia, PA 15044
(40.625514, -80.006635)

Trail: Hike along Blue Mist Trail/Road—1.8 miles, one-way. Out and back. Fairly level. Old road bed. You can hike nearly 1.8 miles to Babcock Road in the Irwin Run Conservation Area, then turn around and hike back. Along the way, explore the ruins of long-gone residences.

Pennsylvania State Gamelands Number 51— Betty Knox Road
Dunbar, Pennsylvania
Fayette County

The Legend of Betty and Her Ox

Betty Knox Road—

There is a road in Fayette County called Betty Knox Road. It is named for Betty, who lived in Fayette County by Kentuck and Tharp knobs around the Revolutionary War from 1775 to 1783. Her mother had died when she was young, and her father raised his only child as any hearty settler would in those old days, training her to farm the land and taking her with him to the mill to grind their grains.

They traveled employing an ox-driven wagon filled with the crops they had harvested to a gristmill in Ferguson Hollow, leaving along a path they had worn with their cart covering the rugged distance. Together, they farmed until Betty's father died when she was hardly out of her teens. Then, she took over the farm and eked out a settler's life without him.

At the time, Isaac Meason, who built Union Furnace in 1791, also owned 6,400 acres of the best coal and iron in Western Pennsylvania that was once the plantation of George Washington's guide, Christopher Gist. Among Meason's other business quests were two local sawmills and a stone gristmill for the grinding of grains. It would be the gristmill that Betty would regularly lead her ox, pulling her wagon full of corn and wheat to grind and garden vegetables to sell in old Union Town. She did not mingle much with the townspeople when she went, although they saw her and the old ox come and go quite regularly and were curious about this quiet, independent woman.

Tongues wagged after she came to town unescorted on her 28-mile round-trip journey. Among them, townspeople whispered that she had always come alone, for she found a wounded British deserter while the war still played out. She nursed him to health, then harbored the fugitive from the British army that would surely hang him for forsaking his post. So that the military did not catch him, he tended the farm while she drove the ox to town by herself.

One day, someone noticed that her routine trips to town had stopped entirely. Authorities in the community sent a search party looking for Betty, but her home was empty, and her animals that had been well-kept were almost starving in the barns and fields. They searched for her everywhere—up and down the roads, along the creeks, in towns, and called out her name— "Betty Knox, Betty Knox!" but to no avail.

That is, until years later, when talk of the woman disappearing and her whereabouts had nearly died down, two boys fishing along a babbling brook found the bones of Betty's old ox tied with a chain to a tree. What had become of Betty? No one may ever know. Some speculate Indians, who were known to harass settlers in the area, might have been the culprits of her vanishing. A cougar or other wild creature may have killed her along the journey to the mill, or thieves may have waylaid her trip.

Along Betty Knox Road where I hiked—

Some say the curious can still find Betty's spirit standing along that old road, just a bit past the place where Betty Knox Road crosses over Tucker Creek and runs along Dunbar Creek where searchers found the old ox. If you are quiet and park your vehicle by the side of the road, you can hear the mournful cry of the old ox ride the misty air until it fades away with the wind. You can listen to the cry of someone calling her name over and over, "Betty Knox, Betty Knox!"

But who is calling her name, you might wonder? I may shed some light on the answer because I went for a visit to see if I could see the ghost and hear the calls. Not long after I turned on Betty Knox Road, I parked my jeep and got out. I waited. I listened. The wind kicked up a bit, and Dunbar Creek was rolling fine after snow and then a thaw. After about ten minutes, I thought I heard laughter and people chattering. It sounded like a church picnic was going on somewhere nearby, but nobody was around. I could not quite make out the words. That is when I heard it—*Betty Knox. Betty Knox.* It was deep, almost frantic, and a man's voice calling out loud in the distance like someone holding cupped palms on either side of the lips and hollering for someone who is lost. It stopped. Did I hear it? *Betty Knox. Betty Knox.* I swore I heard it again surging with the water. Then it occurred to me—could it be the babbling Dunbar Creek bouncing in the wind?

There was only one way to find out, I figured, and that was to follow it. *Betty Knox. Betty Knox.* Again, I heard it. It was almost like I would stop, and there would be a lull, then it would cry out again. I decided to investigate, walked through the thicket of trees and laurels, followed a little stream, and stopped at the creek. I strolled along the bank for an hour or so, took in a good hike, and picked up some glass worn smooth in the water. *Betty Knox. Betty Knox.*

Hmmm. Now it was across Dunbar Creek. What the heck? I went down a little farther and had to veer off to a deer path and away from the creek to get around a tangled mess of laurel and brush. Not once, but twice. Then I thought I heard the calls just a stone's throw away. I was not sticking with the creek, which is my usual mode of mapping, because, as someone has told me more than once, my sense of direction is so bad, I would get lost in a bucket.

I realized that the calling had stopped, and the chuckle of the creek was far away. No. I heard it again but in a different direction. *Betty Knox. Betty Knox.* It was right about then that I got the heebie-jeebies. And yes, I can find a way out of a bucket when I want to because I made it back to my jeep in record time!

What was the calling? I did not think much of it until I brought up the story to a couple of people two weeks later. And here is how the conversation went—

Me: (as if this has happened to me often even though it has not): — "So after I heard somebody calling Betty Knox the last time, I just decided I imagined it. I hiked a couple more hours and then went back to my jeep and left." (I know, I hustled back. In my defense, I was under pressure in the conversation to not be a scaredy-cat since I occasionally boast that I have been to a lot of haunted places.)

The person: "Well, it's a good thing you left."

Me: (feeling uneasy again, but trying not to show it): "Um, Why?"

The other person, with eyes rolling and looking at me like I have never written a folklore book in my life, answered: "Haven't you ever heard of a calling ghost?"

I shudder to think about it now, but I had not. I was quick to find out that it is a spirit that calls to you or calls your name to lure you to your death. I guess on my trip, I was lucky. But, perhaps, Betty and her ox were not.

_____

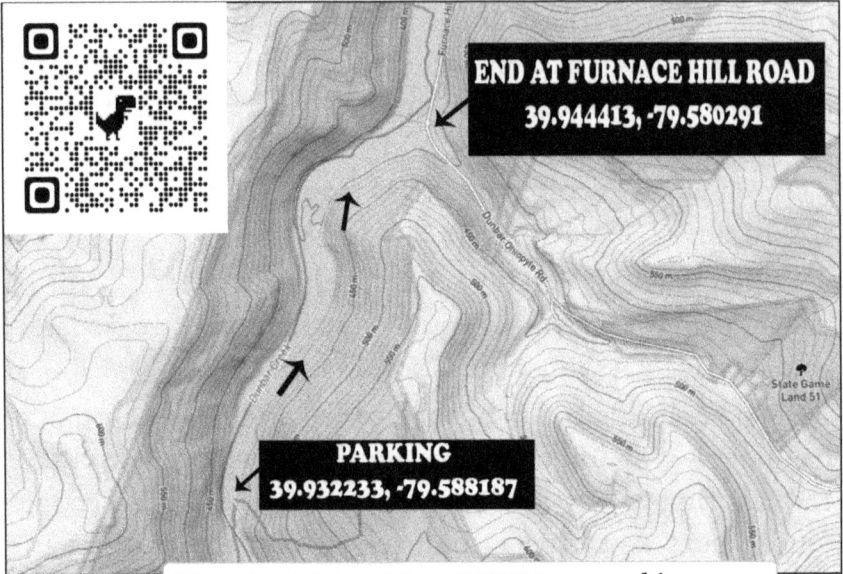

END AT FURNACE HILL ROAD
39.944413, -79.580291

PARKING
39.932233, -79.588187

Map: Open Street Maps/USGS topographic maps.

Parking: There is a designated parking area along the road one mile from Tucker Run/Furnace Hill roads. You will drive along the road to get to the parking, then you can hike back along the gravel road the way you drove, 1.0 mile to Tucker Run/Furnace Hill roads.
Betty Knox Road
(39.932233, -79.588187)

Trail: **Hike Betty Knox (Knocks) Road**—It is within Pennsylvania State Gamelands Number 51. Hike along Betty Knox Road where calling sounds are heard (this road is open for traffic so caution must be taken. 1.0 mile (one-way). Gravel roadway (in use). Out and back. Mostly flat. Side/hunter trails can be explored along the way which lead to the beautiful and bubbling Dunbar Creek.
End at Tucker Run/Furnace Hill roads:
Betty Knocks Road
Dunbar, PA 15431
(39.944413, -79.580291)

McConnells Mill State Park—
Hell's Hollow Trail & Falls
Portersville, Pennsylvania
Butler County

Hell's Hollow & The Legend of Spirit Falls

Within the embrace of Hell's Hollow—left, Hells Run where a dead man was discovered, and right, Hell's Hollow Trail. Both lead to a ghostly conclusion.

There is a lone hollow that was once a part of the hunting grounds of American Indians. As the settlers began moving into this fertile land in the late 1700s, small cabins dotted the landscape, and both settlers and Indians tolerated each other as best they could. In the late 1790s, the Pews were among the families living along a ravine overlooking a dark and narrow gully near what is now Old Sharon Road.

Frequently friendly Indians would stop in for a visit, but one known as Harthegig had a reputation as being a drunk. When he was too intoxicated, he could be quite disagreeable. He was big and ugly, and the Pew children tried to stay far away from him on his visits because he would tweak an ear, pinch an arm, or find some way to bully them.

Hell's Hollow Trail

Samuel Pew was the eldest son of the Pew children. When he was just a young boy, and on one of the visits by Harthegig and two other Indians, he was sitting on a log by the fire warming himself. Harthegig suddenly jumped up, grabbed the boy by the hair, and exclaimed: "I will scalp you!" It so terrified those in the home, including a neighbor James Jeffers who disliked Harthegig, that they all sprang to their feet and disarmed the man of his weapons.

The next morning, Samuel was playing near the home, and James Jeffers passed by asking the boy if he had seen Harthegig. He had. Samuel pointed to the direction of a path the Indian had traveled that morning. Jeffers then disappeared up the same way.

Where the legend of Hell's Hollow sprang up—Spirit Falls.

Harthegig was never seen alive after that day. It was something of a mystery until a passerby discovered a huge skeleton not far away from the Pew home and along a creek nine years later. It was that of the missing Indian. Harthegig's ghost haunts that lone hollow now dubbed Hell's Hollow, and the stream flowing through it, Hells Run. There is a waterfall along a trail fed by that creek where Harthegig's body was secreted, Spirit Falls. Harthegig's dying screams, moans, and groans ride from his lonely grave along the water's path to the falls, and as they run through the rocks to be dumped at the bottom, they are released into the air. If you listen carefully, you can hear them still.

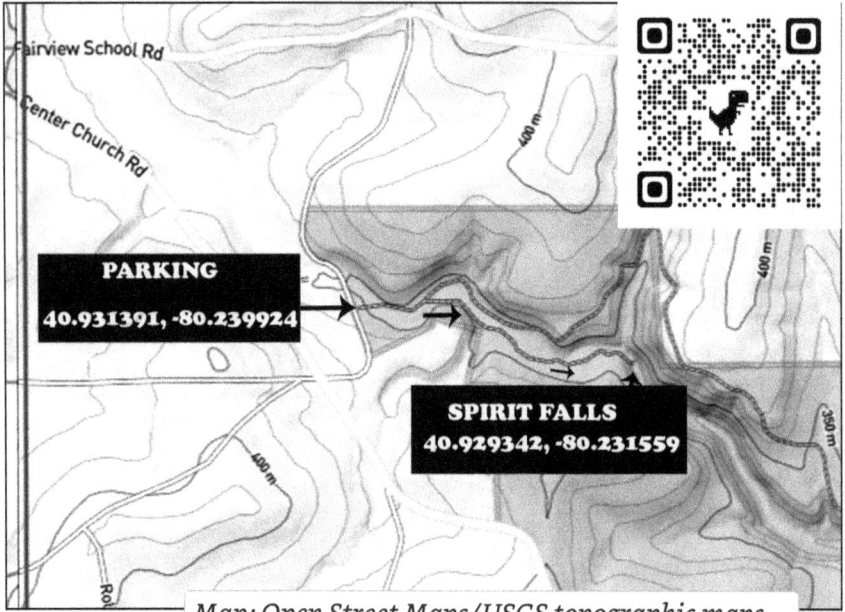

Map: Open Street Maps/USGS topographic maps.

Parking:
There is a designated parking lot at Shaffer Road
Shaffer Road
Ellwood City, PA 16117
(40.931391, -80.239924)

Trail: Hike to Spirit Falls—Hike along the Hell's Hollow Trail that parallels Hells Run (creek) to Spirit Falls: 0.6 miles (one-way). Mostly flat forest trail. Developed Trail. Out-and-Back.

End: At Hell's Hollow Falls.
(40.929342, -80.231559)

Ohio

Hocking Hills State Park

Hocking Hills State Park is located in Southeastern Ohio. It has seven main hiking areas to explore that are steeped in history and wilderness. It has become a major attraction worldwide for its recess caves with cascading waterfalls to hemlock-lined trails through deep gorges. But there is a dark side to this recreation area for the living. It is also a playground for the dead—

Hocking Hills State Park— Ash Cave Trail

South Bloomingville, Ohio
Hocking County

Pale Lady of Ash Cave

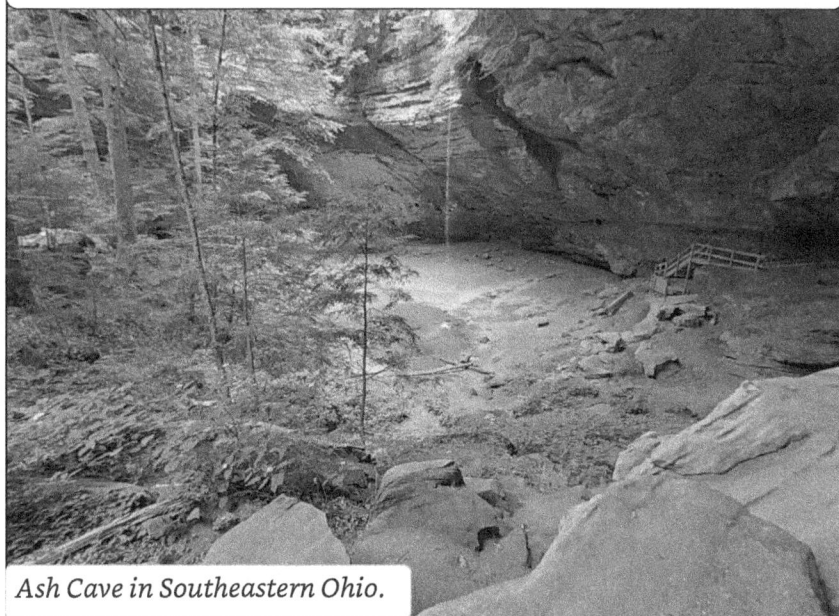

Ash Cave in Southeastern Ohio.

Early one spring, Pat Quackenbush, retired park naturalist, led hikers on a special night tour. It was a short hike along a concrete walkway a half-mile to one particularly large recess in the sandstone called Ash Cave where a waterfall cascaded down a cliff. It was a small group of twelve people, and this night as they walked, he would pause beneath the hemlocks and cliffs and face the group, pointing out some unique features along the route.

Each time they stopped, he would make a quick headcount silently to himself to make sure everyone kept up with him. He did not want anyone lost in the dark! "—*ten, eleven, twelve*—" Once Pat could see he had accounted for everyone, he called attention to a deer almost hidden and grazing in the grass. He then made the perfect imitation of a barred owl's call that, almost immediately, was returned with a couple of hoots from deep in the forest.

He always paused before each stop; there were usually one or two stragglers in the line who would get caught up in the charm of the fairyland-like trail. "—*ten, eleven*," he counted in his head. "*Yep*—*twelve. All there*." And, if needed, Pat would patiently wait for a minute or two, so anyone left behind could catch up before he doled out another trinket or two about the unique area around them.

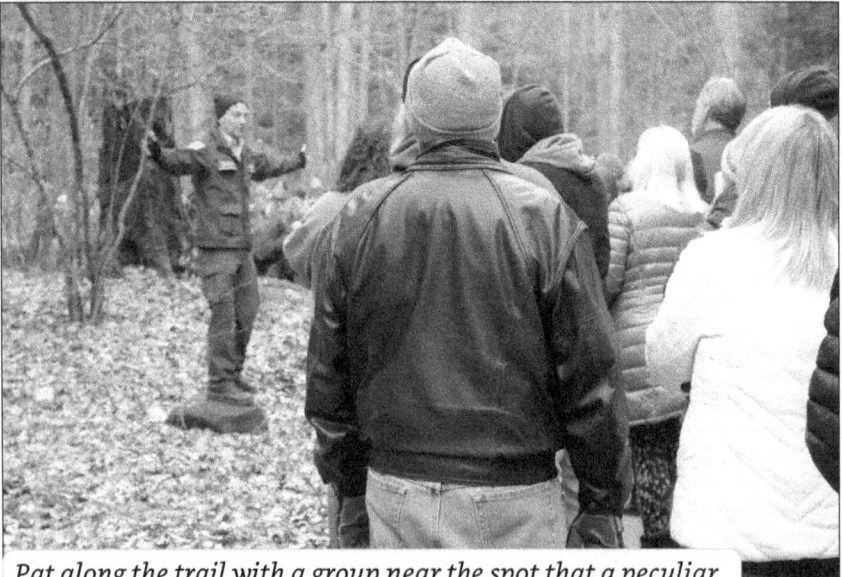

Pat along the trail with a group near the spot that a peculiar hiker has been known to join the group.

About a quarter of the way, he realized that one dawdler had seemed to creep from the shadows right before he started his spiel. "—*ten, eleven, twelve*—*and*," he counted.

"Hmmm, thirteen?" At first, Pat thought perhaps he had counted the number of people wrong when they met. Maybe she had been enjoying the walk alone under the huge hemlocks and wanted some time away from the rest of the group. It was not as troubling that there was one *more* person added to the group than there was one *less*. So instead of waiting and making a recount, the naturalist decided to continue, knowing the straggler would eventually catch up with the group.

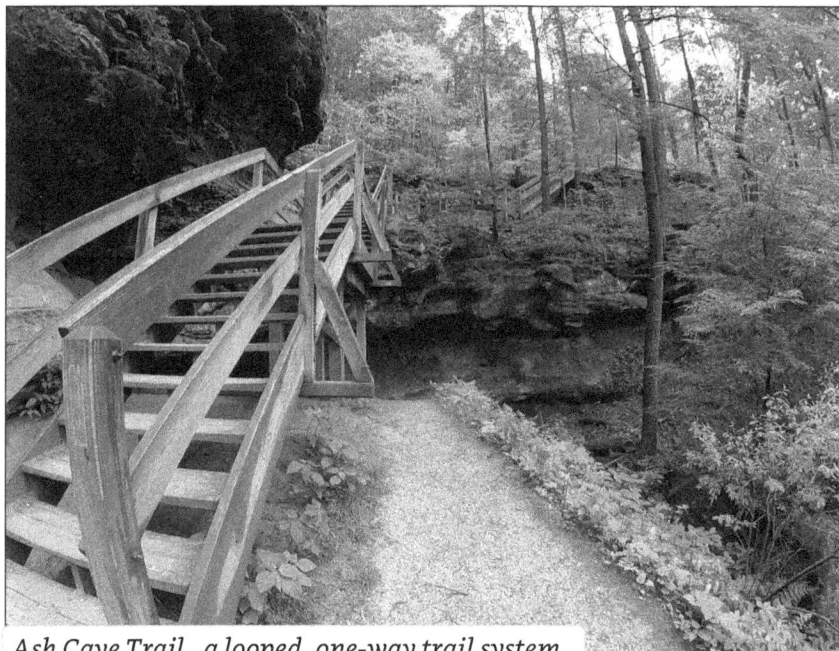

Ash Cave Trail, a looped, one-way trail system.

He was about halfway to the cave when he stopped long enough to talk about an ancient beech tree near the trail. The group had made a half-circle around him, and while they did, he made a great effort to count everyone quickly. *"—ten, eleven, twelve——"* He glanced up and noticed the straggler was only about five feet from the hikers. *"Thirteen!"* He had counted correctly!

But number thirteen was not like the rest. He noted she was wearing old-fashioned clothing—a feed sack dress commonly worn by the thrifty women in the 19th-century depression era who used flour and feed sacks to make their clothing. The mysterious guest was so out-of-place with the group, he was thrown off-guard and simply brought it to everyone's attention. "I turned my attention behind the group," Pat said, "and proceeded to ask if they could see the woman who was standing there and had been following us. I watched them reluctantly turn, and there were more than a few gasps. I wasn't alone. Everyone on that hike saw her." Then she took two steps and disappeared into the woods.

Since then, others have brought the lone hiker that strays behind the group to his attention. Once in a while, witnesses have reported seeing a woman peeking from behind a tree. Then she vanishes from sight.

———————————————————

ASH CAVE

- Ash Gorge Trail
- Ash Rim Trail
- Grandma Gatewood Trail
- Buckeye Trail
- ◆ Waypoint
- Steps
- 🅿 Parking Lot
- Restroom
- Scenic Overlook
- Shelterhouse
- Wheelchair Accessible

Ash Cave

100' Waterfall

**Ash Cave Entrance/Exit
39.396235, -82.545487**

TRAIL ENTRANCE
BEGIN ONE WAY

EXIT ONLY

State Route 56

0   1:3,600

N

Map: Ohio State Parks and Watercraft

Parking: Parking lots—there are two. One is smaller right at the trail and the second is larger and just across the road.
27291 State Route 56
South Bloomingville, OH 43152
(39.395829, -82.545617)

Trail: 0.5 miles. Loop, one-way. Maintained/interpretive. The trail starts near the closer parking lot and loops around. It is one-way for pedestrians and has steps (for those in wheelchairs, it is out and back at the cave). The first half is asphalt and wheelchair accessible. At the halfway point, there is a seasonal waterfall. There are steps past the halfway point.
Trailhead: (39.396235, -82.545487)

Hocking Hills State Park—
Old Man's Cave Trail
Logan, Ohio
Hocking County

Old Retzler's Bones

There once was a quiet town between Logan and South Bloomingville called Cedar Grove. It was settled near a sandstone gorge with a meandering creek that ran beneath the cliffs, called Cedar Creek. Many years ago, two young boys who lived in the town were exploring the valley and its many nooks and crannies. Growing bored after climbing one boulder after another, they built a small fire within a large recess cave that overlooked a valley of hemlocks and craggy rocks.

Old Man's Cave in earlier years.

One of the boys, the younger of the two, was uncertain about visiting this particular cave. It was rumored to be haunted. Some had heard the low baying of a dog at night there, but when they searched for the dog, it could never be found. The boys had only been inside the cave a few minutes when the crunch of footsteps on leaves and sand forced them to look up from the flames. An old man and a large, white dog, staying close to the man's side, walked past them. The man had a long, gray beard, old-fashioned clothing, and leather moccasins. He carried an antique rifle over his shoulder. The man appeared to be interested in the back of the cave. He paced back and forth near the edge of the far rocks and, upon coming to a standstill, peered intently at a shallow depression in the sandstone earth. Then both vanished into the depression as if they had not been there at all!

Eagerly, the boys sought help from some local adults at Cedar Grove in investigating the place the old man had disappeared. With mattocks and shovels, a small crew of men removed rocks and dug out the hollow in the cave's sandstone floor. They exposed two sets of bones: a man and a dog, an old flintlock rifle with the date of 1702 etched into it, and some cooking pots. There was also an scratching in the stone that stated the man's name and the date of his death as 1777. For quite some time, many travelers would come to visit to see the remains inside the cave they dubbed Dead Man's Cave or Old Man's Cave. They would stare down at them and wonder who the man and dog had once been. Some would hear the baying of a hound dog far away, and rumors prevailed that the ghostly dog returned, but for what reason, they did not know. After a while, the bones disappeared. The curious stopped coming, and the story faded away except for a few old-timers living in the community, who brought it up once in a while when lingering outside the grocery store.

Old Man's Cave today.

One late autumn night not too long ago, a park ranger listened intently to the sound of a dog howling deep in the gorge. Occasionally, dogs from the scattering of homes nearby strayed from their backyards. They usually found their way home, but this particular dog sounded like a hunting hound, and the frantic bay most certainly meant it had treed a raccoon. It could mean that poachers were hunting in the park.

The ranger snatched up his flashlight and worked his way down the rugged trail and into the gorge. He followed the sound of the dog, filtering out the splash of a waterfall and the crunch of sandstone at his feet. But even while he got closer to the dog's baleful howls and threw the beam of his flashlight upward, he could see little in the fog flowing up along the rock cliff. He saw nothing but darkness and a rock wall. And yet, the howls got louder and louder until they seemed to be circling him just out of reach. He whipped his flashlight around in a circle, then just as suddenly as the dog's baying came, it ceased.

For years, many have heard the baying of a phantom dog within the gorge and cave area called Old Man's Cave. Its presence is explained as this—

Before the settling of the towns of Logan and Cedar Grove, some trappers lived along Cedar Creek, a stream that worked its way through a deep sandstone gorge. These men made their home in modest one-room cabins or animal-skin tents abutting the small caves within the gorge. They made a living selling the pelts of the many fur-bearing creatures like otter and fox that roamed the region at the time.

As their jobs required them to travel far into the wilderness, they were gone for many days at a time. One winter, upon returning from a seasonal hunt, neighbors noticed that one particular trapper named Retzler, who made his home in a cave outcropping along with his dog Harper had not been seen in quite some time. The usually heavily-traveled path to his abode was overgrown, and there was no sign of his faithful hound who bayed whenever someone neared the camp.

After taking the footpath that led to the cave, they lifted the flap of his leather-hide tent and peered inside. Before them lay the dead trapper along with his old hound dog dead by his side. They carefully lifted the limp bodies of the man and dog and placed them in a shallow hole they had dug in the back of the cave and covered them with sand.

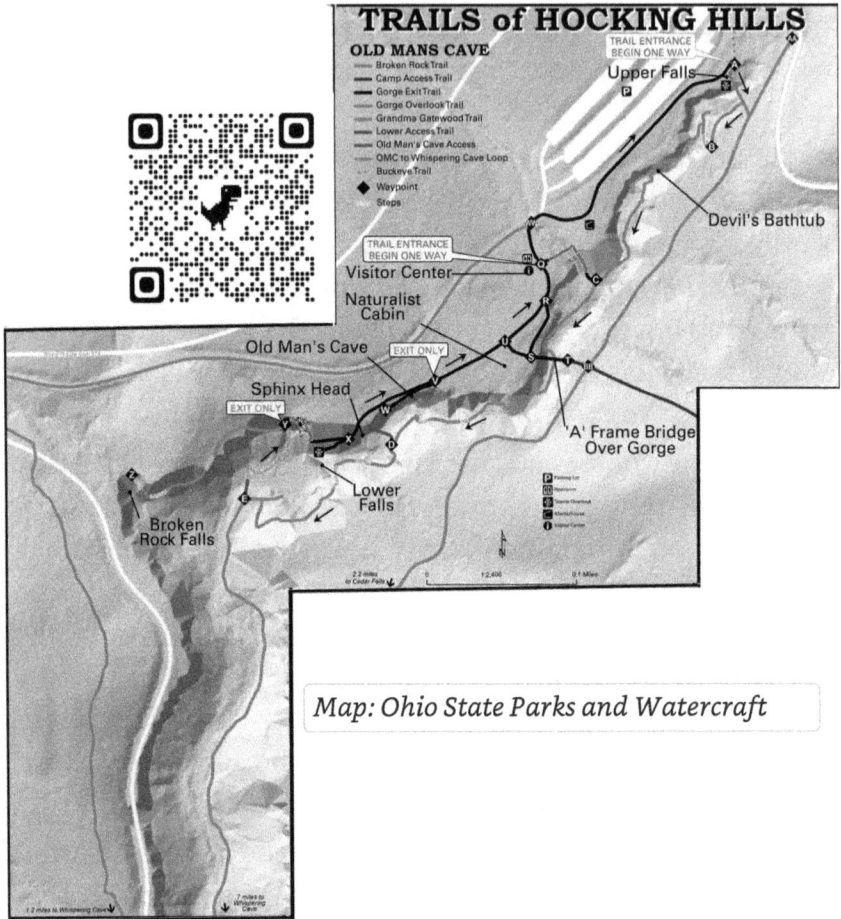

Map: Ohio State Parks and Watercraft

Parking: Designated parking.
20490 OH-374/664
Logan, OH 43138
(39.437687, -82.539339)

Trail: **Hike Old Man's Cave Gorge**—The one-way, maintained loop trail is approximately 1.0 to 1.5 miles long and begins at the kiosk at Upper Falls which is at the Old Man's Cave parking lot. (39.436378, -82.539179)

Hikers can choose from 2 exits:
Exit 1—Cross the stone bridge leading up to Old Man's Cave, continue through the cave and up the steps to the Naturalist Cabin and later, the Visitor Center. **Trail: 1.0 mile**.
Exit 2— Past Old Man's Cave to Lower Falls, following a steep incline with an elevation change at the winding stairway, which ends at the Naturalist Cabin and Visitor Center. **Trail: 1.5 miles.**

The Ghost Town of Moonville

The town of Moonville was little more than a tiny mining community with a few homes and a gristmill along a remote section of railroad and along Raccoon Creek. In actuality, it has gained more celebrity after it became an abandoned ghost town—and one with ghosts—

Moonville—
Moonville Rail Trail
Zaleski, Ohio
Vinton County

The Ghost of Moonville

Moonville Tunnel—

Among the many small mining and railway ghost town communities along the abandoned Marietta and Cincinnati tracks in southern Ohio, one sticks out among the others for its reputation as being haunted. It is called Moonville.

Although it was little more than a bit of land owned by the Ferguson and Coe families, the tracks, trestles, and tunnel that ran through it were used by many travelers to get from one town to the next as a flat shortcut avoiding the hills in the surrounding area. The number of trains and pedestrians sharing the track would make for countless deaths—and more than a few ghosts.

As Moonville outshines other ghost towns in the region as having the most ghosts, one haunting has overshadowed the others and has been documented the longest. That is the death and ghostly return of an engineer in the late 1800s—

Theodore Lawhead was an engineer for the Marietta and Cincinnati railroad company that ran through southeastern Ohio towns like Marietta, Chillicothe, Kings Station, Ingham Station, and Moonville. The route he took cut a path through Ohio's wildest terrains and had numerous tunnels and trestles. Both eastbound and westbound trains shared a single track with passing areas.

One November night in 1880, while Lawhead was heading through southern Ohio, the dispatch failed to notify the eastbound train of the westbound's route and time. As a result, the two collided near Moonville Tunnel, and Lawhead and his fireman died instantly. After the wreck, train crews feared going along that stretch of the railroad. They said they would see the flicker of lantern light when they came along a certain section of the tracks near the tunnel in Moonville. As they got closer, a robed figure would join the lantern light and step out toward the train before vanishing.

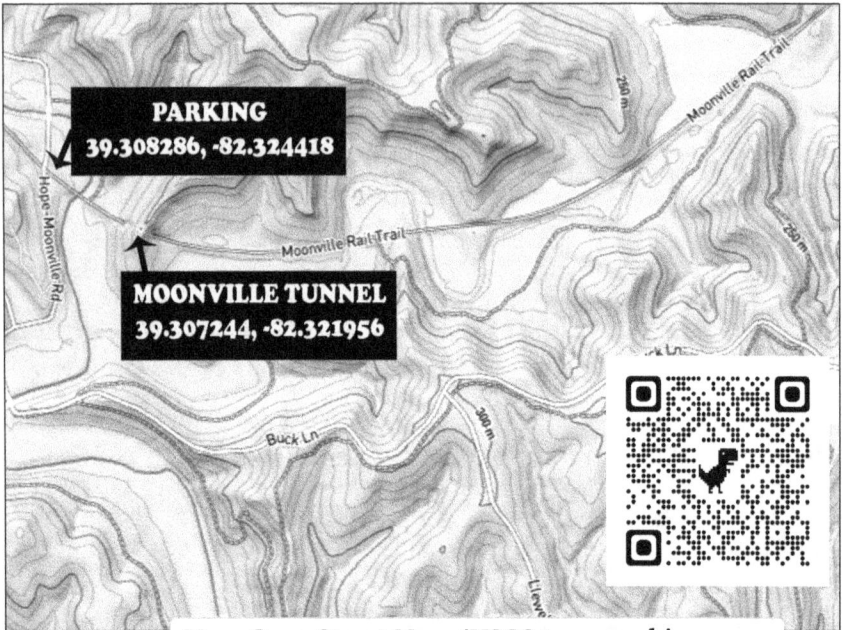

Map: Open Street Maps/USGS topographic maps.

Parking: Designated parking near Moonville Tunnel.
Hope-Moonville Road
McArthur, OH 45651
(39.308286, -82.324418)

Trail: Hike 0.2 miles (one-way) along maintained rail-trail path (Moonville Rail-trail). Mostly flat. Out and back.
Tunnel: (39.307244, -82.321956)

Bear Hollow — Moonville Rail Trail
Zaleski, Ohio
Vinton County

One-handed Shade of Bear Hollow

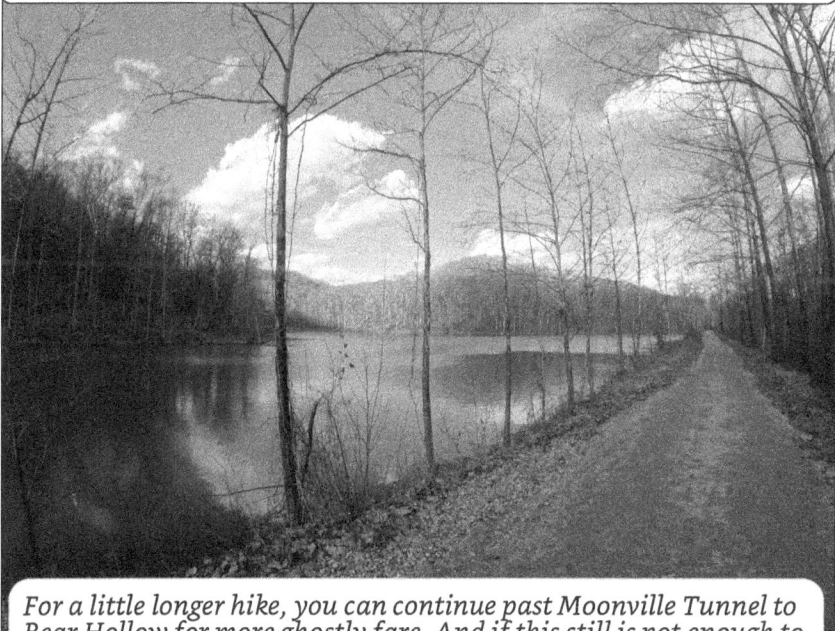

For a little longer hike, you can continue past Moonville Tunnel to Bear Hollow for more ghostly fare. And if this still is not enough to sate your hiking and haunted hiking appetite, you can discover my book—Moonville. Its Past. Its Ghosts. Its Legends. It offers ghosts all along the rail-trail to Kings Tunnel!

The last time anybody saw middle-aged coalminer Allan Albaugh was Saturday, August 24th, 1907. He had been drinking when he hopped on a train at Zaleski with a jug of whiskey in his hand and heading for his home near Athens.

For several days, nobody heard from him, so a search party was sent out to find him. Soon enough, they discovered his hand near Moonville Tunnel.

While walking the tracks at Bear Hollow near Ingham Station, Frank McWhorter smelled something dead and found the rest of Albaugh rotted and covered in maggots. Later, some who walked the railroad from Moonville to Ingham Station said they saw a one-handed man walking the tracks with eyes peeled to the ground. It was Albaugh's ghost searching for his hand.

Map: Open Street Maps/USGS topographic maps.

Parking: Designated parking near Moonville Tunnel.
Hope-Moonville Road
McArthur, OH 45651
(39.308286, -82.324418)

Trail: Hike 1.5 miles (one-way) along maintained rail-trail path (Moonville Rail-trail). Mostly flat. Out and back.
Bear Hollow: (39.310479, -82.302272)

More Trails Around the Appalachian Region of Ohio

Robbins Crossing
Historic Village-Hocking College—
Hockhocking Adena Bikeway
Nelsonville, Ohio
Athens County

Haunted Cabin

A train passes near the Hockhocking Adena Bikeway—as does a ghost.

The Hockhocking Adena Bikeway runs along the old Hocking Valley Railroad bed about 21 miles connecting the towns of Nelsonville and Athens. It begins near the depot of the popular Hocking Valley Scenic Railway, which offers historic train rides, and runs alongside for a short stint. Along the beginning of its scenic route, it passes Hocking College. It is here a haunting transpires. It centers around the historic village of Robbins Crossing and an old cabin built by John and Martha Anthony over 190 years ago on land outside nearby Union Furnace nearly six miles away.

It would still be quietly settled there along with its haunting if it were not for the Nutter Brothers strip mining on Loomis Road in the 1970s. The company was going to demolish the building when they dynamited and bulldozed the property to get to the coal beneath. But the Anthony family, who had lived in the home for generations, donated the building to Hocking College in 1977 as part of a historical teaching complex.

The Anthony Cabin, front, beyond—the Hockhocking Adena Bikeway.

The cabin is unique—a duplex found more commonly in close-knit Appalachian communities than anywhere else. It offered separate quarters for two generations of the family when the parents lived on one side and their grown child and family on the other—a total of four generations living in the home since 1830. There is a ghost. With all the mamas and daddies, kids, aunts, uncles, and grandparents living and loving and sometimes dying at the cabin, it was not at all surprising, even to the family, that somebody decided to stick around after they passed on.

It was not just the family who knew about the ghost. When dismantling the building, some employees of the strip mining company refused to help take down the home. They had seen the ghost on occasion rambling around outside the building—one even going as far to divulge that while he was patrolling the area around 2 a.m., he watched in astonishment as a tall, white ghost drifted from within the cabin and worked its way around the building. Another offered this up about the ghostly presence before the cabin's move to the campus: "I don't want to go up there and tear down that guy's home." But they did tear it down and put it back together at the college to save it.

The Hockhocking Adena Bikeway, and Robbins Crossing, left.

Over the years at Hocking College, staff and visitors have watched as doors open and close on their own. Ghostly footsteps creep across the floor, and voices from the home's long past linger in the air. Sometimes, a pale figure drifts from within the cabin in the dark of night and roams the grounds.

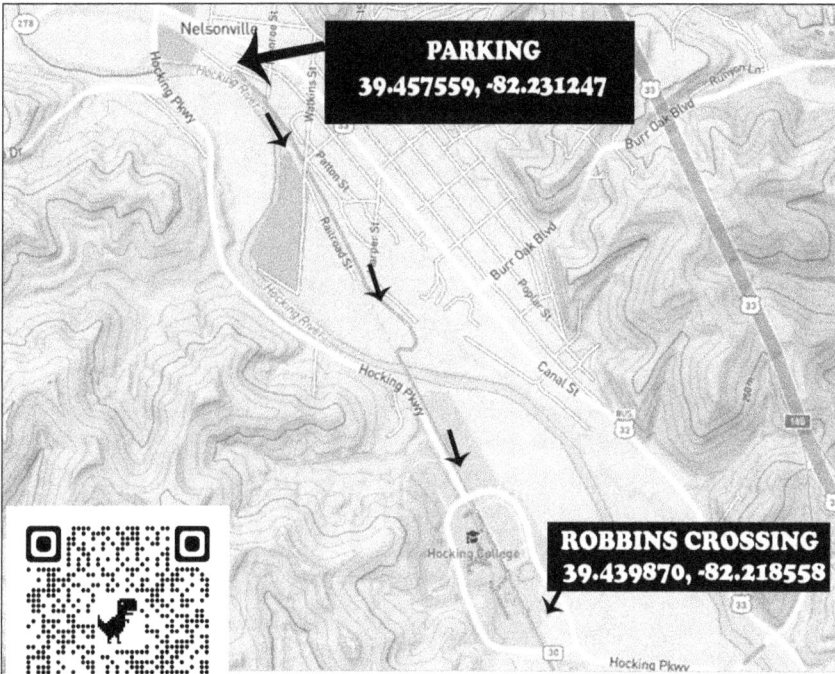

Map: Open Street Maps/USGS topographic maps.

Robbins Crossing

Parking: Designated Rail-trail parking at the rear of **Rocky Boot Outlet.**
45 E Canal Street
Nelsonville, OH 45764
(39.457559, -82.231247)

Trail: Hike the **Hockhocking Adena Bikeway** 1.5 miles (one-way) to Hocking College and Robbins Crossing Historical Village. The Anthony Cabin is marked with a placard. Smooth asphalt surface on rail-trail suitable for hiking, biking, and wheelchairs. Well-maintained.
(39.439870, -82.218558)

Miamiville— Little Miami Scenic Trail Ohio Bicycle Route 3
Loveland, Ohio
Clermont County

Strange Light Bobbing

A ghostly light floats near present Beech Road on the Little Miami Scenic Trail—

Those who walk the Little Miami Scenic Trail near Miamiville occasionally see a strange, dim light bobbing and weaving along the old railroad tracks. Some follow this glow, much like the warm flame within a lantern, only to see it fade away just as it rounds a curve. The cause of the light is explained like this:

In July 1863, John Morgan led Confederate raiders into Ohio. While there, some of his troops came upon the Little Miami River Railroad and built a barricade of cross-ties wedged upright in a cattle guard at a section of the tracks called "the dangerous curve" between Miamiville and Branch Hill. In the early hours of the morning, the Morrow passenger accommodation Kilgour passed through with one baggage car and three passenger cars carrying 150 recruits from the Clinton County militia traveling from Columbus to Camp Dennison. They were less than three miles from their destination, and all were unarmed.

The raiders hid in a cornfield and fired at the train as it passed. Within the locomotive, both the engineer and the fireman were alarmed by the unexpected attack. The fireman aboard the train was named Cornelius Conway. His job was to help watch for signals, but most of all, anticipate how much fuel was needed to feed and stoke the firebox to keep the train running—speeding up or slowing down when needed on hills or in an emergency. At the sound of shots, Conway snatched up a lantern and peered outside, noting the shots were coming from Confederate troops. He knew there was an upcoming blind bend in the tracks and just the right amount of fuel needed adding so that the train could speed up but still negotiate the dangerous curve ahead. Just then, the train rounded the sharp bend and came upon the point where Morgan's men had removed the rails. The locomotive derailed and ran off the track, and the cars detached and went past it with the recruits tumbling out.

These recruits, with bumps and bruises, were captured and released after swearing an oath they would not fight the Confederacy. The engineer suffered a broken collarbone. But Cornelius Conway and his lantern were crushed beneath the train. Conway was buried, but his soul remains at the site of his death, floating along the tracks with his lantern in hand.

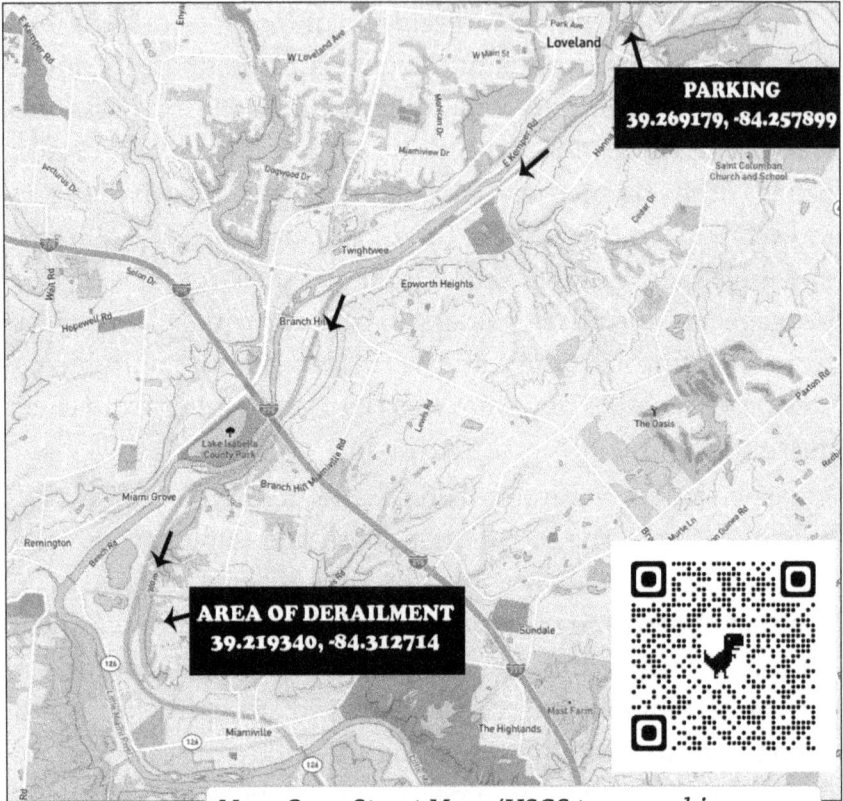

Map: Open Street Maps/USGS topographic maps.

Parking: Designated parking area:
Little Miami Scenic Trail River and Trail Center—
Loveland, OH 45140
(39.269179, -84.257899)

Trail: This is a longer hike as parking areas are limited along the haunted section of the hike/bikeway.

To get to the area of the derailment and where Conway's ghost is seen, hike 4.2 miles (one-way) along the well-maintained rail-trail path to the intersection of Beech Road and the trail. Staying on the trail, cross the road, and walk another 0.43 miles south past the intersection and where it curves (this is the area of the derailment). Around this area: (39.219340, -84.312714) Flat. Out and back.

Beaver Creek State Park— Gretchen's Lock Trail
Calcutta, Ohio
Columbiana County

Along the banks of Strouds Run.

Specters of Old Sprucevale

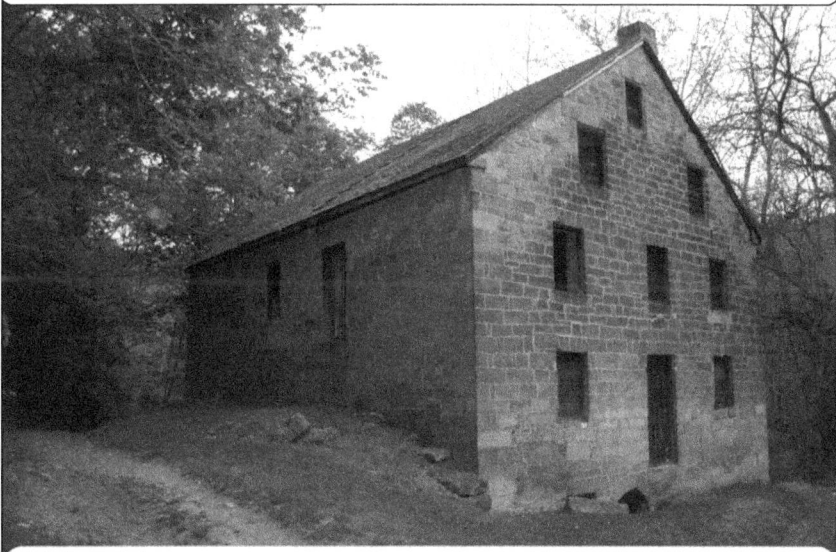

"In the deserted stone mill at Sprucevale, on St. Nicholas eve, the ghost of Esther Hale, the Quaker Lady preacher, appears and rewrites on the stone wall her old text 'Come.'" Ira Mansfield; Robin Hood Club. Little Beaver River valleys, Pennsylvania—Ohio with illustrated check list of flowers and essays. 1914.

The Old Canal Town and Esther Hale—

In the early 1800s, four brothers purchased a gristmill and platted out the town of Sprucevale, which, at its peak, had about 12 homes with 20 families. The 73-mile Sandy and Beaver Canal ran through the tiny prosperous town.

It thrived quite well for its time with a gristmill, pottery shop, woolen factory, store, post office, warehouses, and a blacksmith shop. The community flourished until 1847 when the canal boom years waned with the coming of the railroad and the lack of funds to sustain it. So reliant was the town upon the canal that when it declined, the people and the buildings began to fade away too.

The deserted gristmill remains today, and it is home to the ghost of Esther Hale. Hale came from Carmel Church of the Orthodox Friends. She was among the first of these robust Pennsylvania preachers, a hard worker who toiled among the Sandy and Beaver Canal laborers. She was a tough old bird, frugal, and advised temperance among the rowdy canal men who liked to imbibe in a few drinks after a grueling day of work. Whenever Hale would preach, she would call out for those in her audience: "Follow me down the path to salvation!" Now on St. Nicholas's Eve, December 5th of each year, the ghost of Preacher Hale appears at the old Hambleton gristmill dressed in white. She scratches "Come" on the wall of the old stone gristmill before she leads those watching inside and vanishes.

Gretchen's Lock—

According to old archives, E.H. Gill was the chief canal engineer and a Royal Engineer's School graduate from Paris. He traveled from France along with his wife and 7-year-old daughter, Gretchen, to help build the Sandy and Beaver Canal. Unfortunately, tragedy struck halfway to the United States when waves washed Gill's wife overboard, and she drowned. Grief-stricken, the father and daughter continued to their new life. Gill would get a job with the Sandy and Beaver Canal system and help build the lock above Sprucevale. His daughter followed him from camp to camp, living in the wild area around the new canal.

During this time, Gretchen contracted malaria. One afternoon as her fever mounted, she made her father promise to take her home and bury her with her mother— "I want to join my mother," she pleaded. Wanting to please her, the father nodded that indeed, he would. But, before the day ended, Gretchen was dead.

Temporarily, workers prepared a crypt in the masonry of Lock 41 just above Sprucevale and entombed Gretchen in a small casket there. A major recession in the U.S. economy occurred in 1837, and Gill resigned his position to return to Europe. Her father removed Gretchen's body from her interim tomb in the lock and placed it on the ship to return home for reburial. However, the vessel that Gill was sailing on was lost at sea during a storm on the return voyage. He and Gretchen would join her mother just as she begged him to do. Still, the specter of Gretchen returns to the lock occasionally, murmuring her dying prayer, "Bury me with my mother."

Gretchen's Lock on a rainy summer day with little orbs of raindrops reflecting in the camera flash.

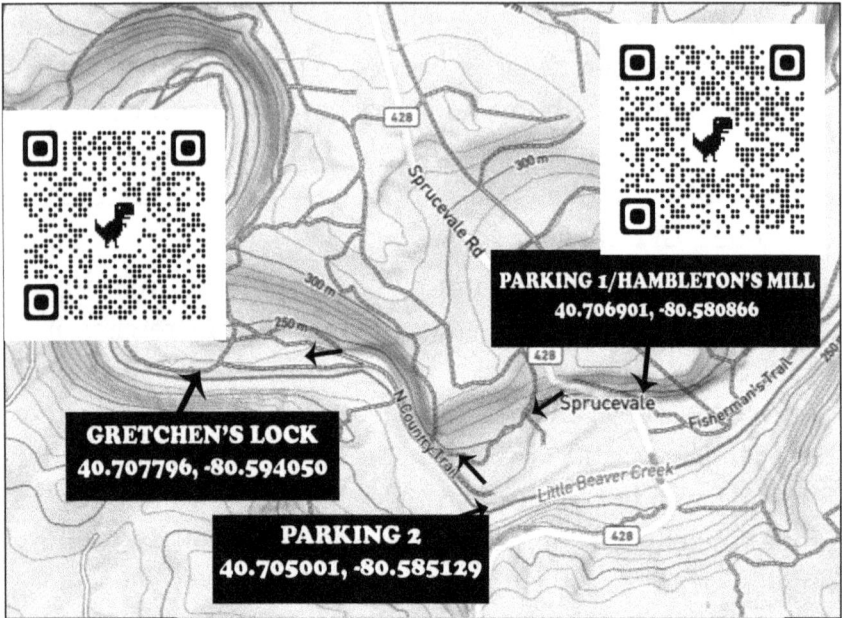

Map: Open Street Maps/USGS topographic maps.

Park: Hikers have two parking area options, depending upon how far they wish to hike. Hike from the Hambleton Mill (about 1.0 mile one-way) and through the parking area, or park right at the trail (about 0.5 miles one-way).

Parking at Hambleton's Gristmill:
Hambleton's Mill (for 1.0 miles, one-way trail)
Sprucevale Road
Negley, OH 44441
(40.706901, -80.580866)

Parking in a lot by the trail:
Beaver Creek State Park Parking (for 0.5 miles, one-way trail)
East Liverpool, OH 43920
(40.705001, -80.585129)

Trail: Hike to old lock. Maintained nature trail. Out and back.
Lock: (40.707796, -80.594050)

Citations

Pennsylvania:
Blue Mist Road/Lovers Graves:
—www.trytoscare.me/legend/blue-mist-road-pittsburgh-pa/
—Pittsburgh Post Gazette October 30, 1994 Folklore of Road Known by Locals
—Pittsburgh Post Gazette VoicesNorth October 30, 1994 Goulish Folklore breeds Legend of Blue Mist Ghost
—https://sites.rootsweb.com/~njm1/03CrossRoads.htm
Betty and her Ox:
—The Daily CourierAug 19, 1974
—The Daily Courier Aug 9, 1919_
—The Morning Herald Wed Feb 25,1925
—The_Pittsburgh Press Jun 3,1923
Dead Man's Hollow:
—Pittsburgh Post-Gazette Pittsburgh, Pennsylvania Thursday, April 06, 2000 - Page 117
P—ittsburgh Daily Post Pittsburgh, Pennsylvania Wednesday, August 03, 1881 - Page 4 DEAD MAN'S HOLLOW
—Pittsburgh Daily Post Pittsburgh, Pennsylvania Friday, August 05, 1881 – Page 4
—The Valley Sentinel Carlisle, Pennsylvania Friday, August 12, 1881 - Page 4
—Pittsburgh Post-Gazette Pittsburgh, Pennsylvania Friday, May 26, 1944 - Page 13
—The Pittsburgh Press Pittsburgh, Pennsylvania Thursday, August 08, 1907 - Page 1
—The Pittsburgh Press Pittsburgh, Pennsylvania Friday, December 01, 1916 - Page 6
—The Somerset Herald Somerset, Pennsylvania Wednesday, March 14, 1883 - Page 2
—https://alleghenylandtrust.org/wp-content/uploads/2016/12/1-Dead-Mans-Hollow-Management-Plan-Final.compressed-1.pdf
—The Pittsburgh Press Pittsburgh, Pa December 01, 1916 - Page 6 INTERPRETER'S BODY FOUND IN CREEK
—Dead Man's Hollow - Popular Pittsburgh. https://popularpittsburgh.com/dead-mans-hollow/
Dravo Cemetery:
—Ghost Stories Haunt Spots on Yough River Trail. (2001, October 31). Pittsburgh Post-Gazette (Pittsburgh, Pennsylvania).
—Mary Ravasio, Tri-State Sports & News Service. (n.d.). Tales of unexplained sights and sounds echo along Youghiogheny River Trail. Post Gazette [Pittsburgh, PA].
—White, T. (2014). Supernatural Lore of Pennsylvania: Ghosts, Monsters and Miracles. Charleston, SC: Arcadia Publishing.
—White, Tom. (2002, October 22). Ghost sightings park of local legend. Pittsburgh Post-Gazette (Pittsburgh, Pennsylvania).
—Gresham, John. Biographical and Historical Cyclopedia of Westmoreland County, Pennsylvania Page 618
Hell's Hollow:
—29 Oct 1977, 23 - Pottsville Republican at Newspapers.com. (n.d.).
—Brown, R. (1888). History of Mercer County, Pennsylvania: Its Past and Present, Including ... Portraits and Biographies of Pioneers and Representative Citizens ; Statistics, Etc. ; Also, a Condensed History of Pennsylvania.
—Hell's Hollow Wildlife Adventure Trail. (n.d.). Retrieved from https://www.visitpa.com/region/pennsylvanias-great-lakes-region/hells-hollow-wildlife-adventure-trail

—Robert-P-Worst - User Trees - Genealogy.com. (n.d.). Retrieved from https://www.genealogy.com/ftm/w/o/r/Robert-P-Worst/WEBSITE-0001/UHP-1251.html

Presque Isle Storm Hag:
—10 Creepy Urban Legends From Pennsylvania Not For The Faint Of Heart. (2015, April 1). Retrieved from https://www.onlyinyourstate.com/pennsylvania/pa-urbanlegends/
—Retrieved from http://www.examiner.com/examiner/x-4872-Pittsburgh-Paranormal-Examiner~y2009m4d17-The-Lake-Erie-Storm-Hag-demonic-siren-of-the-Great-Lakes
—Hunting for shipwrecks in Presque Isle's Misery Bay. (2018, March 8). —
—Retrieved from http://www.rockthelake.com/buzz/2018/02/hunting-for-shipwrecks-in-presque-isles-misery-bay/
—Jenny Green Teeth : Internet Archive. (n.d.). https://archive.org/details/donald_002
—The Lake Erie 'Storm Hag', demonic siren of the Great Lakes. (n.d.). Retrieved from http://theparanormalpastor.blogspot.com/2009/04/lake-erie-storm-hag-demonic-siren-of.html
—Nearby Attractions to Erie Bluffs State Park. https://www.dcnr.pa.gov/StateParks/FindAPark/ErieBluffsStatePark/Pages/NearbyAttractions.aspx

Old Man's Cave
-The Democrat-sentinel., August 12, 1909
-The Democrat-sentinel., August 15, 1907
-The Democrat-sentinel., February 25, 1909
-The Democrat-sentinel., March 28, 1907 Interesting Story of Old Man's Cave
-The Hocking sentinel., June 22, 1905, Image 4 old man hid money

Moonville Tunnel:
Frank Mace Archives, 1961
Mike Shea Archives, 1959-1961
Vinton County Historical Society—Alice's House
Athens Messenger, 2/17/1876
Athens Messenger, May 20, 1880
Athens Messenger and Herald, September 1907
McArthur Democrat, March 31, 1859
Athens Messenger, July 17, 1873
Athens Messenger, Thursday November 11, 1880
The Portsmouth Times, December 27, 1938
Athens Messenger, Thursday, October 16,1873

Little Miami Scenic Bike Trail:
Cahill, L. S., & Mowery, D. L. (2014). *Morgan's raid across Ohio: The Civil War guidebook of the John hunt Morgan heritage trail.* Lulu.com.
Tennessee:

Tennessee:
Big Ridge State Park:
-Big ridge state Park. (n.d.). Retrieved from tnstateparks.com/parks/big-ridge
-Ghostly hikes at big ridge. (2019, September 17). Retrieved from https://www.historicunioncounty.com/article/ghostly-hikes-big-ridge
-The haunted hike in Tennessee that will send you running for the hills. (2016, October 30). Retrieved from https://www.onlyinyourstate.com/tennessee/haunted-tn-hike/
-https://www.youtube.com/watch?v=jFhTZrrjicw
-The Herald-News Passaic, New Jersey Tuesday, October 31, 2000

Smoky Mountains:
-Park spawns spooky stories. (n.d.). Retrieved from https://archive.knoxnews.com/news/local/park-spawns-spooky-stories-ep-410821030-359724961.html-Bales cemetery, Sevier County, Tennessee, US: Smoky mountain ancestral quest. (n.d.). Retrieved from https://

www.smokykin.com/tng/showmap.php?cemeteryID=10
-Bradley, M. (2016). Death in the great smoky mountains: Stories of accidents and foolhardiness in the nation's most visited Park.
-Cultural comparisons. (n.d.). Retrieved from https://www.handsontheland.org/hands-on-history/cultural-comparisons/details/53/49-bear-trap-accident.html
-FamilySearch catalog: Smoky mountain clans — FamilySearch.org. (n.d.). Retrieved from https://www.familysearch.org/search/catalog/185808?availability=Family%20History%20Library
-Giles P. Reagan B. Jun 1882 Sevier County, Tennessee D. 16 Sep 1933: Smoky mountain ancestral quest. (n.d.). Retrieved from https://www.smokykin.com/tng/getperson.php?personID=I1704&tree=Smokykin#cite2
-Giles Permon Reagan. (n.d.). Retrieved from https://www.findagrave.com/memorial/8390481/giles-permon-reagan
-Jasper Mellinger B. Mar 1837 Ohio D. 1901: Smoky mountain ancestral quest. (n.d.). Retrieved from https://www.smokykin.com/tng/getperson.php?personID=I2922&tree=Smokykin
-Mountain Man Caught in Bear Trap, Dies of Starvation;Dying Boy's Tale Leads to Finding of Skeleton Years Later. (1923, December 22). Knoxville News [Knoxville].
-Smoky Mountain Historical Society. (1984). In the shadow of the Smokies: Sevier County, Tennessee cemeteries.
-Some of the Richest History Lives in Legends. (n.d.). The Knoxville News Sentinel Mar 5, 1978.
-Russell, R., & Barnett, J. (1999). *The granny curse and other ghosts and legends from East Tennessee*. Blair. (Cades Cove Cussing Cover and Lucy of Roaring Forks.)

Elkmont:
Elkmont ghost town: Smoky mountain tales that will give you goosebumps. Story by Melinda, former worker. (2021, October 28). Retrieved from thesmokies.com/elkmont-ghost-town/
Everything you need to know about Elkmont ghost town. (2020, June 22). Retrieved from https://www.visitmysmokies.com/blog/smoky-mountains/about-elkmont-ghost-town/
Everything you need to know about Elkmont ghost town. (2020, June 22). Retrieved from https://www.visitmysmokies.com/blog/smoky-mountains/about-elkmont-ghost-town/
NPS story map journal. (n.d.). Retrieved from https://www.nps.gov/gis/storymaps/mapjournal/v2/index.html?appid=ba52cfb987704b91bc32479b864c7edc
-The eerie ghost town in the Smokies. (2021, October 29). Retrieved from https://thewellwornshoes.com/daisytown/

West Virginia:
Harpers:
General
-Bluefield Daily Telegraph may 6, 1984
Dougherty, Shirley. A Ghostly Tour of Harpers Ferry. EIGMId Publishing.
-Brown, Stephen D. Ghosts of Harpers Ferry
Silver Run
-Anthony, Reevy. "Stories of Railroad Ghosts." *National Railway Bulletin Volume 59 No. 1 1959*, n.d.
Seneca Rocks—Snowbird
-The Weirton Daily Times Mon Feb 28 1955 Legend of Seneca Rocks Remains Alive in State
Droop Mountain Battlefield State Park —
www.droopmountainbattlefield.com/
-The last sleep - Charleston Gazette -www.wvgazettemail.com/News/201311090049

-The Battle of Droop Mountain https://www.mycivilwar.com/
battles/631106b.html
-Cincinnati Enquirer (1872-1922); May 28, 1881; After Eighteen Years—
Description of the Battle of Droop Mountain, West Virginia
-Porterfield, Mannix. Cumberland Evening Times October 28, 1985 -
Ghosts Come Out All Year 'Round in West Virginia.
Cumberland Times News. October 28, 1985.
Maryland:
-Retrieved from https://mht.maryland.gov/secure/medusa/PDF/
Washington/WA-II-1126.pdf
-Maryland heights - Blue Ridge Mountain. (n.d.). Retrieved from https://
www.peakbagger.com/peak.aspx?pid=25662
-National Park Service (NPS) cultural resources plan, H30(2255),
September 12, 1997 (Letter). (1998).
-Norman, M. (2008). Haunted homeland: A definitive collection of North
American ghost stories. Macmillan.
-Then & now: Explore Fox's gap at south mountain battlefield. (n.d.).
Retrieved from https://john-banks.blogspot.com/2017/11/then-now-
explore-foxs-gap-at-south.html
-Tom Lobianco News-Post Staff. (2016, March 11). History unearthed in
south mountain. Retrieved from https://www.fredericknewspost.com/
archives/history-unearthed-in-south-mountain/article_867b12ac-be0f-
5eff-bf0b-a3a4cb430da3.html
-Commentary: McDonogh teachers set Antietam story straight.
(2016, November 3). Retrieved from https://apgnews.com/
community-news/features/commentary-haunted-sites-
antietam/
-WA-II-1126 Wise Farmstead Architectural Survey File. (n.d.). Shows
Wise Property. Retrieved from https://mht.maryland.gov/secure/
medusa/PDF/Washington/WA-II-1126.pdf
Virginia:
-Amherst County Virginia heritage page 131. (n.d.). S. E. Grose.
-David Benavitch, Jodi Barnes, Hugh Bouchelle, Ryan Stowinski. (2021,
October 31). Episode 2: What came before. The Green Tunnel - A podcast
on the history of the Appalachian Trail. https://greentunnel.rrchnm.org/
episode-2-what-came-before/
-Get maps. (n.d.). USGS Topoview. https://ngmdb.usgs.gov/topoview/
viewer/#14/37.6143/-79.3161
-Get maps. (n.d.). USGS Topoview. https://ngmdb.usgs.gov/topoview/
viewer/#15/37.6309/-79.3148
-Https://books.google.com/books?
id=JnVL7wtOLgUC&pg=PA145&lpg=PA145&dq=Nannie+Gilbert+virgini
a&source=bl&ots=afwXxZ7mSL&sig=ACfU3U08HlNW_hvUAwFJthLYsrr
VxsINMA&hl=en&sa=X&ved=2ahUKEwiB4NS3srL1AhWmGDQIHSRsD1
4Q6AF6BAgUEAM#v=snippet&q=little%20ottie's&f=false.
(n.d.). Amherst County Virginia heritage. S. E. Grose.
-Hupp, T. A. (2008). Children lost in the mountains. iUniverse.
id=ePuvFX0g3lcC&pg=PA12&lpg=PA12&dq=Emma+Belle+Powell+virgin
ia&source=bl&ots=cMgsFxM0S1&sig=ACfU3U2LnGBXSI6MuyJ0wH8GAk
ZjDfo0UQ&hl=en&sa=X&ved=2ahUKEwicnrD6t7L1AhXPLcOKHVIHBqo
Q6AF6BAgbEAM#v=onepage&q=Emma%20Belle%20Powell%
20virginia&f=false
-Little Ottie Cline Powell. (n.d.). The Delbridge's Website. https://
www.delbridge.net/ottiepowell
-Little Ottie Cline Powell. (n.d.). The Delbridge's Website. https://
www.delbridge.net/ottiepowell

-Wheeling Register, November 9 1891
-Alexandria Gazette April 6, 1892
-Richmond Dispatch December 15, 1891
-Richmond Dispatch April 8, 1892
-StauntonVindicator November 27. 1891
Corbin Cabin:
-George Corbin interviewed by Edward Garvey, transcribed by Victoria M. Edwards. (n.d.). Retrieved from https://commons.lib.jmu.edu/cgi/viewcontent.cgi?article=1023&context=snp
-Potomac Appalachian Trail Club, "Corbin Cabin Work Trip (1953)," Appalachian Trail Histories, accessed March 4, 2022, https://appalachiantrailhistory.org/items/show/93. (n.d.).
Sarver Shelter:
-https://nps.maps.arcgis.com/apps/webappviewer/index.html?id=6298c848ba2a490588b7f6d25453e4e0
-John Carlin's Virginia Hike to Sarver Cabin and interview of great grandchildren of the Sarver's.
-Tate, J.R. Walkin' with the Ghost Whisperers: Lore and Legends of the Appalachian Trail
-Image of Sarver Homestead: Earl Palmer Appalachian Photograph and Artifact Collection, Ms1989-025, Special Collections and University Archives, Virginia Tech, Blacksburg, Va.
North Carolina:
Spearfinger:
-Retrieved from https://www.firstpeople.us/FP-Html-Legends/UtluntaTheSpear-finger-Cherokee.html
-Asheville Citizen-Times, Asheville, North Carolina, 05 Oct 2017, Thu · Page D4. (n.d.). The Ogress and the Chickadee.
-The Charlotte Observer, Charlotte, North Carolina, Wed, Oct 27, 2004 · Page E2. (n.d.). Spearfinger's Many Disguises.
-Cherokee Legend. (n.d.). Asheville Citizen-Times Asheville, North Carolina Mon, May 20, 1991 · Page 7.
The Fiddler:
-George/Henry grooms - Groom's tune - Newspapers.com. (2000, February 23). Retrieved from https://www.newspapers.com/clip/10099173/georgehenry-grooms-grooms-tune/
-Henry grooms. (n.d.). Retrieved from https://www.findagrave.com/memorial/59391765/henry-grooms
Sarah Jane (Franklin) grooms (1829-1895) | WikiTree FREE family tree. (2018, October 22). Retrieved from https://www.wikitree.com/wiki/Franklin-10667#_note-JFdc

www.ingramcontent.com/pod-product-compliance
Lightning Source LLC
Chambersburg PA
CBHW032347280326
41935CB00008B/479